# ONE-DAY CRICKET

## PLAYING THE ONE-DAY GAME

# ONE-DAY CRICKET

## PLAYING THE ONE-DAY GAME

### ADAM
# GILCHRIST

with John Townsend

HarperSports
An imprint of HarperCollinsPublishers

## *Authors' note*

This book is written for cricket players and fans alike: young or old,

male or female but, for the sake of simplicity, we have referred to certain

positions as batsmen, fieldsmen, and so on.

**Harper*Sports***
An imprint of HarperCollins*Publishers*, Australia

First published in Australia in 1999
by HarperCollins*Publishers* Pty Limited
ACN 009 913 517
A member of the HarperCollins*Publishers* (Australia) Pty Limited Group
http://www.harpercollins.com.au

**HarperCollins*Publishers***
25 Ryde Road, Pymble, Sydney, NSW 2073, Australia
31 View Road, Glenfield, Auckland 10, New Zealand
77-85 Fulham Palace Road, London W6 8JB, United Kingdom
Hazelton Lanes, 55 Avenue Road, Suite 2900, Toronto, Ontario M5R 3L2
*and* 1995 Markham Road, Scarborough, Ontario M1B 5M8, Canada
10 East 53rd Street, New York, NY 10022, USA

National Library of Australia Cataloguing-in-Publication data:

Gilchrist, Adam.
One-day cricket: playing the one-day game.
ISBN 0 7322 6713 7.
1. Cricket. 2. One-day cricket.
3. Cricket – Rules. I. Townsend, John. II. Title.
796.358

**Photographic Credits**
Unless individually credited, all internal photography by Malcolm Fairclough,
with the exception of page 81 inset by Shaun Botterill/Allsport, and page 177
inset by Ben Radford/Allsport. Front cover by Michael Dodge/*Herald and Weekly Times*;
back cover by Ross Kinnaird/Allsport.

The statistics published in this book are correct at the time of going to press.

The extract on page 31 from the 1986 edition of *Wisden Cricketers' Almanack*
is reproduced by kind permission of John Wisden & Co. Ltd.

Printed in Australia by Griffin Press Pty Ltd on 79gsm Bulky Paperback

5 4 3 2 1    99 00 01 02

# Acknowledgements

Several people have had a big influence in the writing and completion of this book. In this regard I would like to thank John Townsend for the many hours he contributed, his influence on how the book was written and his enthusiasm for the whole project. I would also like to thank my manager, Stephen Atkinson, for the fantastic ideas he provided and for his continued support; my wife, Mel, for her great support and assistance – both for this book and in everything else that I do; Steve Waugh, for the wonderful foreword and for his belief in my cricket; and many thanks to my father, Stan, to Tom Moody, Nick and Kidda Stagg, and Malcolm Fairclough for their valuable input into various sections of the book.

Finally, thanks to Alison Urquhart and the team at HarperCollins*Publishers* for their enthusiasm and support.

# Contents

# Foreword

There's a bit of a story as to how Adam Gilchrist first came to open the batting for the Australian one-day side. It was during a one-day international against South Africa in Melbourne not long after I had first been appointed captain of Australia's one-day side, at a time during the summer of 1997–98 when our performances hadn't been all that encouraging. There was much debate going on about the merits of having different Test and one-day sides, and about what the best Australian one-day batting order was. For this match, Tom Moody was to open up with my brother Mark, but during the dinner break between innings it suddenly occurred to me that our new keeper/batsman might be the man for the job.

'Gilly,' I asked, 'how do you feel about opening up?' A more expected question would have been, 'Gilly, can you please pass the salt.' It really was that impulsive a decision on my part, but he didn't bat an eyelid.

'Yeah, I'll give it a go,' he quickly but quietly replied.

And then he went out there and, typical of his one-day batting career to date, approached the task with a very positive attitude. Today, he is one half — Mark Waugh being the other — of the best opening partnership in international limited-overs cricket. And Gilly is arguably the most dangerous one-day opening batsman around.

In many ways he encapsulates the future of one-day cricket. These days you have to be excellent in at least two of the three facets of the game — batting, bowling and fielding — and Gilly really fits into that mould, as a world-class one-day opener and wicketkeeper. You could call him a 21st century all-rounder. As a keeper, Gilly has a perspective on the game that most other cricketers don't get. In most games, from very early on he's on his own, with no slip fieldsmen to keep him company. He has to concentrate for every ball. Better than anyone, he knows how the bowlers are going. As a captain, I need his advice quite often, to make sure the field placements are right, that the boundaries are as difficult to reach as possible, to find out exactly what the bowlers are doing. How hard is Glenn McGrath hitting the bat? Is Warney spinning it far? Is Flem getting any swing?

The keeper is also best placed to gauge the tempo of the game, and advise whether we should be slowing things down, or picking up the pace. And he is the trendsetter on the field, setting the mood for the outfielders. If a keeper is down on form, almost inevitably the entire team fielding performance will suffer.

Gilly first came into the NSW team in 1992–93, as a specialist batsman, filling in for guys such as Mark Taylor, Mark Waugh and myself who were often away on Test duty. We were rarely, if ever, in the same XI, so I didn't get to know him that well, even though we were both technically wearing the baggy blue cap, until he made the Australian squad. His selection in the Aussie one-day squad came after he had moved to Perth, to take over the WA wicketkeeping job, and it was only then that I discovered how much he'd fulfilled the early potential he'd shown in Sydney, and what a good cricket brain he possessed.

Now he's a World Cup champion. For much of the Cup tournament he struggled a little with the bat, but because he worked hard on his game and listened to the advice of the right people around him, he came good in the final against Pakistan. Before that game, all the media talk was of the 'Rawalpindi Express', Shoaib Akhtar — would he smash the 100mph barrier? — and the skill and reverse swing of their captain Wasim Akram. But Gilly murdered them, smashing an incredible 54 from 36 balls as we won emphatically in just 20.1 overs.

*One-day Cricket: Playing the One-day Game* captures the fact that limited-overs cricket has changed dramatically through the '90s, even in the last couple of years, as more one-day 'specialists' emerge. It offers a fascinating insight into the way the Australian one-day side prepares for battle, shows how young cricketers can improve their game, and gives fans a genuine appreciation for the many intricacies of the limited-overs game. There's something for the young cricketer, the park cricketer, and something for the international cricketer, too. Showing what a clear and clever thinker he is about the sport, the book's thoroughness demonstrates not only why Gilly is such a good one-day player, but also why he will be a valuable Test-match cricketer of the future.

*Steve Waugh*

# Introduction

'Just go out there and play your natural game.' Steve Waugh's instructions rang in my ears as I walked out to bat. 'Play your natural game and back yourself,' he said. It seemed so simple, yet few words carry the weight of that plain advice. I had to play my natural game. There was no point trying to bat like anyone else. I had to use the approach that had got me to this level. If the ball was there to be hit, I was going to have a go at it.

It was January 23, 1998. I had played 18 one-dayers for Australia – mostly as a middle-order batsman, but also as Australia's wicketkeeper in the last eight games after replacing Ian Healy at the start of the summer. Stepping into the Test record-breaker's shoes was a big task, but this was my toughest challenge yet. I was about to open in the first final of the Carlton and United Series against South Africa in Melbourne.

It was not something that I had had a lot of time to worry about. In fact, I was still savouring my effort behind the stumps earlier in the day when I took two catches and two stumpings – still my equal-best one-day haul – when Tugga came up to me during the dinner break.

His question came out of the blue. 'How do you feel about opening up?' he asked. 'I might go with you today to open with Mark.' I almost dropped my bowl of ice cream. It was the first time I had considered opening and in less than an hour, I would have to go in against Allan Donald, Shaun Pollock, Brian McMillan and Lance Klusener – a quartet of quality quicks, the fiery engine-room of the powerful South African team.

I didn't have the chance to think about what could go wrong. If Steve Waugh thought I was capable of opening, and he was a player who had been up against the best in the world for more than a decade and had played more than 200 one-dayers, there was no reason for me to panic. He must have seen something in my game that gave him confidence and that flowed back to me.

It wasn't such a strange move, anyway. Australia had tried Michael Di Venuto, Stuart Law, Jimmy Maher and Tom Moody in eight games that summer without settling on an opening partner for Mark Waugh. Now that Mark Taylor, his opening partner of 25 games and several campaigns, was no longer playing one-dayers, Australia was looking for a pair capable of providing the regular and long-term role that had been the hallmark of the two Marks, as well as David Boon and Geoff Marsh in the late 1980s and early 1990s.

Play your natural game ... I was in the middle of the MCG. Forty-four thousand people were watching. Pollock was bowling with the new ball ...

I had cracked three in a row just behind point but couldn't get it past the most exciting fieldsman in the world – the rubber ball wearing the shirt labelled 'Jonty Rhodes'.

Crack. Another ball was in the slot. Just short enough to step back and give it a full swing. But again Jonty moved like a streak of lightning to pick up the ball before I could run.

'Right,' I thought. 'The next one goes. No matter what happens, I'm off.' The ball was short. Again it flowed from the bat and I set off. But Jonty was too quick. Out of the corner of my eye I saw Mark Waugh hesitate then start to stretch out as Jonty swooped. Too late. The throw went to Pollock who, in a flash, relayed it to Richardson who whipped the bails off with Junior well short of the crease. He trudged off without looking at me, but he didn't have to. I knew exactly what he was thinking, let alone the names he was calling me under his breath.

I had to work hard for the next few overs, but managed to get 20 before scooping a catch to Pat Symcox off Pollock. Steve Waugh and Michael Bevan then combined to almost get us across the line but we fell just six runs short of South Africa's 241.

Three days later, we worked better together to form a solid Australia Day partnership. Mark got a typically elegant 25 and I scored 100, my first in Australian colours, as we successfully chased South Africa's 228. And if I was rapt with my innings, spare a thought for Geoff Marsh, now our coach. Swampy, who scored 9 one-day tons mostly as a sheet-anchor at the top of the order, was so happy that another West Australian had joined the century club that he leapt from his seat and belted his knee on a table – giving himself a serious injury and providing considerable mirth for my teammates.

Play your natural game. I had and the reward was there for all to see – a ton in front of a packed house at the SCG in my twentieth game for Australia.

Play your natural game. The advice is simple, yet of all the suggestions you hear from coaches and supporters, it is the most important. Sure, one-day cricket demands that players are versatile and capable of improvising as the occasion requires, but as I found when I got thrown in at the deep end to open the innings in a MCG final, you have to learn the fundamentals and then apply them to your own skills and attributes.

Hopefully, this book will help you do that.

3

# The 1999 World Cup

Can anything beat the feeling of winning the World Cup? If so, I don't know what it is.

In the space of two short weeks, the Australian team went from being down and out against South Africa, to scrambling an amazing tie in the best game of cricket I have ever played in, to beating Pakistan in the World Cup final at Lord's, to being the centrepiece of tickertape parades in Melbourne and Sydney. It wasn't a dream – we have the trophy to show how real it was – but I wonder if anyone would have imagined the twists and turns we experienced on our path to victory or realised how overwhelming the response to the win was going to be.

It probably took until the first tickertape parade in Melbourne for the enormity of what we had done to sink in. In fact, that half-hour we spent on the back of cars driving past 100 000 or so cheering Melburnians provided me with the proudest feeling of my sporting career. It made me feel I was the luckiest person alive and that all of Australia had come together to celebrate and unite as one, much as the team itself had done during the business end of the World Cup.

As we passed those smiling, happy faces, it actually felt like much more than a World Cup had been won. I felt like it gave so many people the chance to temporarily forget any problems or hardships they had and celebrate the wonderful country we live in and the spirit we possess. There were youngsters of just two or three right up to grandparents, all seeming as though they had played a part in the success of the team.

5

I remember as a young bloke watching Australia play and living and breathing every ball and moment of tension. I rode every high and fell with every low of those matches and remember the awesome adrenalin rush whenever Australia won a match. It was a proud feeling as if, just by watching and supporting and urging on the team, I had played a part in the victory.

I'm sure I felt that same emotion among the people taking part in those two magnificent parades – in their smiling, green-painted faces and in their cheering and laughter. The proud, never-say-die Australian spirit was flowing freely among the coloured streamers and showed that what we had done was more than just win the World Cup – it was as if all of Australia were winners, too, and proud to be a part of it.

# That Match

There are three things people want to talk about when the subject turns to the 1999 World Cup – THAT shot, THAT ball and THAT tie.

The first is my top-edged cut shot off Shoaib Akhtar in the final at Lord's that flew high over second slip and crashed into the advertising boards at third man. That six has become the most talked-about shot of my career. Though it may not have been as well hit as Doug Walters's famous hook shot to bring up his century in a Test against England at the WACA, or the huge blow Kim Hughes launched onto the Lord's pavilion in the Centenary Test in 1980, it seems to have generated almost as much attention. I'll talk more about that later.

The second is THAT ball – the unplayable delivery Shane Warne produced to bowl South African opener Herschelle Gibbs in the semi-final at Edgbaston. I had the best seat in the house to observe that delivery. Luckily it hit

6

the off-stump because it was on its way for four byes if it had missed!

The ball swerved at least 50 centimetres towards the batsman's pads, leaving me stranded down the leg-side when it snapped back that far again to bamboozle Gibbs and cannon into his stumps. Warne's bowling had been getting better and better throughout the World Cup, and he started to bowl more aggressively as his confidence and form returned. That ball signalled that he was back to his best. Most significantly, he had produced the deceiving drift that has been such a feature of his bowling in his prime.

It is the best ball I have ever kept to (though Glenn McGrath's superb off-cutter to bowl Brian Lara in the World Cup match at Old Trafford was not far behind it). There isn't a batsman in the world who is fully comfortable against a ball that moves a metre sideways in the air and off the pitch. Warne exploited it with marvellous spells in the semi-final and final that brought him four wickets in each game.

The other thing that people are interested in, of course, is that incredible tie with South Africa in the semi-final at Edgbaston. As I mentioned before, that was the best match in which I have played, pipping the previous match with South Africa three days earlier at Headingley, and took to a new level the intense rivalry that has developed between Australia and South Africa.

It was the 39th match between the two countries and, not surprisingly, the record could not be closer – 19 wins apiece plus that one tie. It is also quite intriguing that while our records are identical, Australia has managed to win the most important games.

We lost the first final in the two triangular series in which South Africa played in Australia in 1993/94 and 1997/98, but bounced back each time to win the next

7

two finals and the series. We were down 2–4, but levelled the series on their home turf in 1994, and came back from 1–2 down to win 4–3 in 1998.

The only blemish came at the Commonwealth Games final for the gold medal at Kuala Lumpur in 1998 – but that match that has not been recognised as an official one-day international by the relevant authorities. So, our record of never losing a series to the Proteas remains intact.

Going into the 1999 World Cup, the two teams were favourites to play off for the title and though it didn't quite work out that way, our two heavyweight matches were probably the best games in the tournament.

But what about that match?

I was reasonably happy with my 20 with the bat after having a pretty quiet tournament. I thought I hit the ball well in that short innings and I have no doubt it set me up for a good knock in the final. While that was at the start of the match, it was the end that will be remembered for many years. Just as people recall what they were doing when they heard about the tied Test against the West Indies in Brisbane in 1960/61, I think thousands of fans will have a crystal-clear recollection of the match that produced what I reckon was the best one-day finish ever.

Everyone has a story about it – wherever you mention the World Cup, that is what people talk about. I have heard so many stories about people sitting up in bed listening quietly to the cricket by themselves and then waking the whole house up with their yelling and excitement as the game finished. I guess it just shows how important cricket is to so many people and that they rise and fall with the fortunes of the national team.

After our great win at Headingley in the previous match – where Steve Waugh played his best one-day

8

innings to score a magnificent 120 not out, including some dynamic slog-sweeps that he had used against the South Africans in that final in Kuala Lumpur – we were full of confidence going into the semi-final at Edgbaston.

Even with the tempo in the match changing regularly – first one team, then the other getting on top – we thought we were a good chance to win. When South Africa were nine down with nine runs to win and six balls to go, we were confident. The only fly in the ointment was Lance Klusener, who swings the heaviest bat in world cricket harder than any other player and can strike the ball to every part of the ground.

Our biggest hurdle in pre-match planning was deciding where to bowl to Klusener – he was equally strong on front and back feet and on both sides of the wicket. Yet with South Africa needing more than one a ball, even with Klusener having clobbered 23 in just 12 balls, we were confident that if we could just get him off strike and attack Allan Donald, we would be right.

The first ball from Damien Fleming was on a good length just outside off-stump. BANG. It went like a rocket through the covers for four. Plenty of players throughout history have hit the ball hard, but this was something else. It scorched across the turf and gave the sweeper on the boundary no chance to move even the 5 metres needed to cut it off. Our emotions dipped. But South Africa still needed a run a ball and we stuck to the plan, hoping that we could get Donald on strike.

Fleming bowled again. It was another reasonable delivery, right on off-stump, but it held no fears for Klusener. Swinging his bat like an executioner with an axe, he crashed it through the covers. It went straighter but took no less time to smash into the fence.

In a few seconds, it looked as though our dream had evaporated. We had been on a rollercoaster of

9

emotion – up one minute, down the next – as we realised how close we had come to achieving an ambition ever-present in Australian cricket since the loss to Sri Lanka in the previous World Cup final in 1996.

But the game wasn't over yet and we thought we still had a chance, slim though it was. Fleming went back over the wicket – quite a telling move as it turned out – and Waugh brought the field in to stop the single. So often that is just a token effort, but this time it worked.

I remember Warne and Paul Reiffel in the slips saying a tie was good enough to get us into the final. But with four balls to go, and the bloke on strike at 31 off 14 balls, it was not something you would have bet on.

The third ball saved us. Klusener hit it firmly straight to mid-on. But with Donald haring down the pitch, he didn't budge from his crease. As the frantic Donald tried to scramble back, Darren Lehmann threw at the bowler's stumps but was just wide, allowing the tailender to make his ground.

If Klusener had run, I'm sure he would have made his ground and it would have been stumps for us. But he didn't and the mix-up must have put seeds of doubt into the minds of the pair, causing them to make a fatal error.

Normally in a tight situation like this, the batsmen would have a quick conference mid-pitch to clarify matters. They would have cleared up any confusion, determined who was going to call and what their tactics would be. After all, they had three balls to get one run and there was no need for panic.

But Klusener and Donald did not have a chat. Instead, they stayed at their ends and prepared for the next delivery without knowing what the other intended to do. Despite their great experience, the pressure of the situation had obviously got to them and they forgot to do something that was so simple, yet so important.

The next ball from Fleming, who had kept his head superbly despite the load resting on his shoulders, was straight and Klusener could only force it firmly back down the pitch to mid-off. This time, Klusener took off – he thought Donald was going to go. Donald stayed – he thought Klusener would play it like the previous ball and not run. Havoc reigned.

At mid-off, Mark Waugh swooped and picked the ball up as clean as a whistle before backhanding it neatly to Fleming beside the stumps. Fleming turned slowly and produced the simplest relay of the ball you could ever see.

He rolled it along the ground underarm to my end, and though it seemed to take forever to get to me, once I had it in my glove and had the bails off, it was as if a bomb had gone off inside me and the entire team as we celebrated our amazing fortune.

Actually, I wasn't sure what happened then, but after watching four or five replays, I finally realised that I set off for the far end, ignoring the stumps in front of me, to grab a couple of souvenirs.

In any historic moment, you want to get hold of a momento – which is why I charged to the other end, almost knocking umpire Venkat out of the way, to grab the stumps. It was probably the right decision, too, because the stump I eventually got has a shiny white mark near the top where Warne had bowled Gibbs earlier.

I have also been asked what happened to the ball. Well, about 20 minutes after we won, I was sitting in the change-rooms with the entire team. We were getting our heartrates back to normal and starting to contemplate our achievement in a rational manner. I looked down into my right glove, which I hadn't yet taken off, and there it was. I have no idea how the ball had stayed there for so long, but it was as tangible and as sweet to hold as the victory itself.

11

It didn't stay there much longer though – Steve Waugh came up to me and asked if he could have it. As much as I wanted to keep the ball from the greatest one-day match ever played, I couldn't refuse the skipper – after all, we would not have been there if it wasn't for his effort in the previous game.

Although the tie was the highlight of my career, as I'm sure it was for many of the other players, we knew we still had a job to do, so we quickly turned our sights to Lord's.

Throughout the tournament, we had had a deep belief in ourselves being able to go all the way and this stunning finish merely reinforced that thought pattern. Even in the early days when we had lost two of our first three games, we did not panic, despite having to win seven games in a row to grab the World Cup. My own form had parallels to that of the team, but again, I did not feel any need to panic despite my poor start to the event.

In both cases, Steve Waugh played a big part in keeping the focus on what we had to do and not becoming sidetracked by concerns about achieving it. In my case, Waugh and coach Geoff Marsh simply reminded me to play my natural game, not focus on getting a big score, and that the runs would come.

We struggled a bit as a team, partly a legacy of a tough tour of the West Indies preceding the World Cup, as well as taking some time to adjust to the conditions in England. After three games, we had just the one win and some people must have been worried that we weren't going to get through to the business end of the tournament.

But we had a big boost in our aggresive run chase after Pakistan's 275 at Old Trafford in the third match. We lost that match, but the way we went about chasing Pakistan's big total gave everyone confidence that we were capable of winning if we played to our potential. This is where Waugh was so astute and provided great leadership – he identified the positives in that tight loss, generally praised the team for its effort and seemed quite at ease with our position. Although we knew there were no second chances if we lost a match, the pressure helped us to switch on and lift to the level at which we needed to play.

Going into the final, we were battle-hardened and ready for the kill. Far from causing us to peak too early, those two extreme matches against South Africa helped us to relax and to believe in ourselves just that bit more. It may not quite have been a belief that we were destined to win, but we were sure Pakistan would have to play exceptionally well to have a chance against us.

So it proved. Our bowlers were superb, with Warne and McGrath never letting their batsmen out of a headlock. The catching was spot-on and the ground fielding tight and aggressive. When it was our turn to bat, we wanted to be equally aggressive to make sure there were no stumbles in the chase for the small target.

While I was happy with my 20 against South Africa in the semi-final, I was annoyed at cracking one to Allan Donald at third man when I was seeing the ball well and moving my feet nicely. That ball from Jacques Kallis probably bounced a fraction more than I expected. The ball hit closer to the edge than the middle of the bat and therefore went finer than I intended. Even so, I was keen for a good knock at Lord's. I was happy with my keeping during the World Cup and I have found that when one aspect of my game is going well, the other usually follows.

This brought me to the battle with Akhtar, who quickly showed he meant business with a rip-snorting bouncer to me, first ball. I had scored a century against Akhtar, in a match in Lahore in 1998, but he cranked his pace up to 155 kilometres per hour on the biggest stage in world cricket to produce the fastest spell of the tournament.

I didn't play the first ball well, top-edging a cramped hook shot just short of fine leg. But I was happy that I had gone with my natural instincts – that is the only way to play a bowler who generates such pace. If you try to predict what he is going to do, or try to read him off the pitch, you are bound to run into trouble.

An over or so later the ball I had been waiting for arrived – a short delivery outside off-stump that I could cut away over point. Leaning back, I gave it everything I could muster, but again, didn't quite catch it in the middle of the bat.

This time, instead of the ball carrying to third man, Akhtar's extra pace gave it enough oomph to fly straight over the boundary at third man. His next ball was full and, playing forward, I hit it sweetly though mid-on where it ran away for four. Ten in two balls but, more importantly, the Pakistanis seemed to drop their heads a fraction as though the reality of their poor score had sunk in and they realised we were going to make the target.

So we did, and the World Cup was ours.

# The History of One-day Cricket

Cricket has come a long way since the game's masters decided 40 years ago, almost in desperation, that the sport needed a revamp if it was not to wither and die. Falling crowds and dwindling income were causing cricket to die a slow death. A radical solution was required to save the game.

Little did the administrators who introduced the first one-day competitions in England in the early 1960s realise the impact they would have on the sport. Would they have believed that not too many years later a one-day player wearing a coloured uniform, and playing at night under lights with a white ball, would wait for an umpire sitting in the grandstand to determine from a television replay whether he was in or out?

That might have seemed revolutionary a few years ago, but it is commonplace today. So, too, the fielding restrictions that determine only five players can be outside the 30-yard circles after 15 overs.

Restrictions were first used in World Series Cricket's one-day matches in the 1977/78 and 1978/79 seasons, along with other innovations such as microphones in the pitch and a reporter waiting to interview batsmen as they walked from the field after being dismissed. The pitch mikes stayed but the reporter didn't last long – sticking a microphone under the nose of one disgruntled batsman after another soon became a health hazard.

But the restrictions were formalised due to the actions of one captain and one ball. Like Trevor Chappell's infamous underarm delivery, it took only one ball for people to realise that a loophole in the rules had to be closed for the benefit of all players, then and well into the future. Those 30-yard circles are the legacy of a stunning tactic used only once by England captain Mike Brearley during a match against the West Indies in Sydney in November 1979. England had not even adopted coloured uniforms like the other countries, but there was no denying Brearley was ahead of his time when it came to innovative and successful tactical thinking.

England scored 8–211 from their 50 overs and the Windies, after a short rain delay, were set 199 to win off 47 overs. With one ball to go and three runs needed, they still had a chance to pull off the victory.

Instead, Brearley pulled a rabbit out of his hat. As the West Indies batsman and the millions watching on television gazed in astonishment, Brearley sent every fieldsman, including wicketkeeper David Bairstow, to the boundary to stop any chance of a four. It didn't matter in the end, because last man Colin Croft was bowled by Ian Botham. Even so, that one ball had a far-reaching impact. To stop it happening again, restrictions on the number of fieldsmen allowed outside specially marked circles were introduced the next season and have since become an integral part of one-day cricket.

Like so many innovations in cricket that are simply recycled from an earlier age, the tactic had been used successfully before. Sixteen years earlier in the first-ever Gillette Cup final at Lord's, flamboyant English batsman Ted Dexter led Surrey to a nail-biting win over Worcestershire by sending all his fieldsmen to the fence for the frenetic last two overs. Perhaps Brearley recalled that incident. Maybe he thought of his plan on the spot. Either way, it doesn't matter other than to

16

demonstrate another example of the evolution and revolution brought by one-day cricket.

Not only did one-day cricket save the game itself – taking it to a new audience and producing a spectacle on a par with any sport – but it has been at the forefront of the very way cricket is played. Night matches? Fielding restrictions? The clever slower ball? Audacious running between wickets? Reverse sweeps? They are all the legacy of one-day cricket and have helped produced a game that, far from swamping the traditional Test and first-class arena, has enhanced and revitalised the sport to the point that it has more players at all levels, more spectators and more interest than ever before.

And it has developed in many directions – from the Kanga cricket matches played by youngsters that are designed to engender enthusiasm for the sport by ensuring everyone gets a go, to the Super 8s and Cricket Max matches that are hybrid versions of the game.

The one-day matches played today are vastly different to the 65-over competition that appeared in England in May 1962. This was the first official attempt to have first-class teams regularly play matches in one day and to restrict the number of overs each team could receive. Restrictions on bowlers were also introduced, through the maximum was set at 15 overs each and even that was done away with during the final of the fledgling Midlands Knock-Out Cup in 1962.

Nonetheless, one-day cricket had arrived and it was explored further during the next ten years as the Gillette Cup (60 overs), Sunday League (40 overs) and Benson & Hedges Cup (55 overs) were introduced.

An eight-ball, 40-over version was introduced in Australia in 1969/70 for the six states and New Zealand, but this took many years to be popularly accepted. Now, of course, the Mercantile Mutual Cup is an integral part of the

Australian domestic calendar. The increasing profile of one-day cricket is also reflected in expanding competitions at club level.

Early games were more like mini Test matches – openers were sent out to blunt the attack, bowlers aimed to take wickets rather than restrict runs – but even then strategies were starting to evolve that can still be seen today. Certainly there was a flurry of hitting in the last few overs that was identical to an innings today.

The first international one-day game was played in January 1971 at the MCG – most appropriate given that 'the G' is the home of cricket in Australia and the site of the first Test match way back in 1877. The match was played here to make up for the washout in the Ashes Test match. Even so, both teams played their Test teams and applied virtual Test tactics to the reduced format.

Opposing quick bowlers Graham McKenzie and John Snow employed three slips and a gully, batsmen crafted their innings gradually and then played orthodox shots to build the score. Indeed, John Edrich, the dour English left-hander, won the Man of the Match award for his solid 82 in England's score of 190. And it comes as no surprise that Geoff Boycott eked just 8 off 37 balls.

Compare that with today's one-day openers, such as Shahid Afridi, who scored a century off only 38 balls against Sri Lanka in Nairobi in 1996; or Sanath Jayasuriya, who clobbered one in only nine more balls against Pakistan in Singapore that same year. Australia won that first game comfortably by five wickets with more than five overs to spare but more importantly, as the crowd of 46 000 indicated, this was no novelty but an innovation with far-reaching potential.

That was certainly recognised by the most influential figure in the game. Writing in the 1970/71 *Australian Cricket Yearbook*, Don Bradman said: 'One-day matches seem destined to play a larger part in our future program.' How true were those words, yet it took nearly five years for the new form of the game to gain wide acceptance. Only 18 international matches were played around the globe in the next four years, and even they were widely condemned by traditional cricket-lovers as nothing more than tasteless slogathons.

The real turning point came with the success of the inaugural World Cup in 1975, and particularly the superb final in which the West Indies beat Australia by 17 runs. From the moment in the first over when Roy Fredericks hooked Dennis Lillee for six but stood on his stumps in doing so, to the frenetic finish in which last-wicket pair Lillee and Thomson tried to run the 20 needed for victory as the crowd invaded the field, the game was full of highlights and spoke loudly of the potential of this new form of cricket.

It was an event described by John Woodcock, the highly regarded but intensely conservative *Times* cricket writer, as 'a piece of theatre: of drama, tragedy, carnival and farce ...' Not a bad way to describe one-day cricket, too, because it regularly displays all those elements and plenty of others as well.

Once one-day cricket got a foothold at that World Cup, it was only a matter of time before it grabbed the public imagination and became a fully fledged fixture of the cricketing summer. Other countries started to host matches – Pakistan in 1976, then the West Indies a year later. Surprisingly, it took until 1981 for India to host its first one-day international – and it had played in two World Cups by then. It has made up for that since then and now only just trails Australia as the country to have played most one-day matches. No doubt they will pass us in the next year or so.

By 1981, of course, the biggest innovation to ever reach cricket had arrived. Cricket at night. Cricket under lights. Matches at which the crowds had stars above them and stars in front of them. Almost by accident, night matches started during the World Series Cricket revolution in 1977/78.

The breakaway venture hired the then VFL Park in Melbourne, which had lights in place for football, and it was a natural reaction to test if cricket could be played as a night sport.

The first match was played on December 14, 1977, and by the time the first game was played in Sydney before 45 000 people a year later – after Kerry Packer had spent $1.3 million to erect light towers at the Sydney Cricket Ground – it was clear the new form of cricket was the way of the future.

Some things had to change, though. That first match at the SCG saw the West Indians, who went down to Australia for the first time, decked out in uniforms described by the promoters as 'strawberry mousse'. That colour didn't last long, but night cricket quickly proved to be far more attractive and long lasting.

The matches were such an immediate and wonderful success that they clearly showed the way of the future. Players had to adjust to the conditions, but the buzz and excitement of playing night cricket ensured it was here to stay. The adrenalin rush of walking out to bat under lights before a packed house at the SCG or MCG has to be one of the great moments in any sport.

In the early days of night cricket, there was a theory that the ball would move around more because of the heavier atmosphere, but that is not really the case. In fact, conditions are reasonably even between day and night except that batsman probably prefer to bat in natural light rather than the white light of a ground under lights. The general train of thought is that batting under lights is more difficult, but I wonder if that is because you are chasing a target. Chasing is invariably harder than setting a target, so perhaps it is just a coincidence that batsmen think it is more difficult at night. After all, visibility is very good at most grounds that have lights and history continues to prove that good batsmen will score runs no matter if they are playing during the day in England or under lights in India.

The only ground at which the lights are much of a problem is at Mohali in Chandigarh. That's the hometown of the great Indian all-rounder, Kapil Dev, and the scene of Australia's miraculous World Cup semi-final win against the West Indies in 1996. It is also right next to an air-force base, so instead of having tall and efficient towers like at the WACA or MCG, it has 18 low towers that unfortunately shine into the eyes of the batsmen and fieldsmen. Although you can see the Himalayas from the ground, there are times when you can't see the ball!

With cricket under lights came other innovations. Traditional red balls were difficult to spot against the night sky, so experiments were carried out to find a ball that could be seen. After orange and yellow were rejected, white became the preferred colour, and that is now virtually universal throughout the one-day world. And because the white balls still became discoloured, separate balls were used from each end – meaning they stayed harder longer and could be hit harder longer. That regulation was scrapped in the mid 1990s and we now play with just the one ball.

And if you can use a white ball and lights, why not coloured clothing? It looks good on television and a bit of razzamatazz can't harm the game.

Coloured uniforms, night matches, white balls, television replays and third-umpire decisions, bowling and fielding restrictions ... these are all elements of the game that have evolved as one-day cricket has grown from strength to strength.

While evolving techniques have brought in reverse sweeps and slower balls, what about the changing tactics that have altered the look and the style of the game? The mini Test match formula has vanished, to be replaced by specialist one-day teams playing this specialised form of the game. Yet like Test cricket and every other form of the game, getting off to a good start is essential. Instead of the luxury of building

21

a solid foundation through patience and grit, modern one-day cricket demands quicker scoring and allows fewer opportunities towards the end if too much time has been used up in early defence. It is a matter of degrees, but most teams now have at least one attacking batsman in the first pair.

Some go even further. The Sri Lankans are a prime example of a team that starts by scoring quickly and then consolidating as it loses wickets. It can get away with that strategy, particularly in the subcontinent, where the ball is easier to hit when it is hard and new and the field restrictions are in place. Later on in the innings, the fieldsmen are on the boundary and the ball is softer so it is harder to score fours.

Australian and English teams tend to play more in the traditional mode that suits the conditions in these countries. Sure, they are aggressive early because a great start of, say, 0–100 in 12 overs sets the base for a big score. But that is not an everyday event, so we are more likely to have a controlled hit early, work hard on running and rotating the strike during the middle overs, and then have wickets in hand to launch an onslaught in the last five or ten overs. There are subtle variations within these parameters but Australia, certainly, has picked up ideas and tactics to broaden the approach that has brought it reasonable one-day success over the past two decades. We will examine some of these tactics in more detail in this book.

And having looked at where one-day cricket started, it is clear that it is now an integral part of the international cricket calendar. It certainly hasn't detracted from the credibility or appeal of Test cricket and, if anything, it has made the longer version of the game more respected and successful. The great thing is that one-day cricket has introduced the sport to a completely new audience and ensured that the battle between leather and willow remains as intriguing as ever.

# Batting

It is imperative to grasp the fundamentals of batting before trying to launch an assault on a one-day line up. It is a simple progression. If you can play a forward defensive shot well, you can carry it through to a good cover drive. And once you have mastered the cover drive, it is a simple matter of developing it that one step further so that you are able to hit over the infield in typical one-day fashion.

But slogging it in wild cross-bat fashion over cow corner? This approach might bring runs once or twice but will invariably lead to your demise sooner or later. Being able to adjust your batting to combat different conditions and styles of bowling or field positions is essential. It is part of the improvisation to which Bradman referred and is probably the key to success in the one-day game.

As Bradman and other good judges acknowledge, succeeding as a good one-day batsmen does not rely on brute strength, but brains, technique and a good dollop of daring.

The basic approach to the task of getting bat on ball doesn't change whether the bowlers are wearing

A SOLID FORWARD DEFENCE PROVIDES THE FOUNDATION FOR ATTACKING STROKES LIKE THE LOFTED COVER DRIVE.

coloured or white uniforms, or whether four slips are in place or four men are on the boundary. Good cricket shots will still be rewarded and the deliveries that get hit for six will still require the eyes on the ball, a full swing of the bat and a good follow-through.

What makes good one-day batsmen stand apart is not their different technique, but their different approach to batting. It is aggression that identifies them – not only Jayasuriya-like aggression in which the ball disappears back over the bowler's head, but also the aggression of a player like Michael Bevan, for example. Bevan is not a big exponent of massive blows over the infield, but rather an expert in clever placement, audacious running and inventive strokeplay. Bevan puts the acid on the bowlers just as much as Jayasuriya does, and though he might not hit many sixes, you can virtually guarantee that he will score off nearly every ball he faces. If a team scores at that same run-a-ball rate that Bevan does, it will win 99 per cent of its matches.

**Michael Bevan**
Born 8/5/70
119 matches 105 innings 41 not out 3822 runs
108* highest score 59.71 average 3x100 26x50

Aggression in running and placing the ball was one of the great attributes Bob Simpson brought to the

Australian team when he became coach in the mid 1980s. Simpson had been a fine opener 20 years earlier, and with Bill Lawry formed a highly successful partnership based on good running, clever shot selection and canny placement. Surprise, surprise, they are exactly the same attributes that define a good one-day batsman today.

Simpson and Lawry developed a great understanding. One of their strengths was the ability to rotate the strike — both in an attacking manner to frustrate the bowler and force him off his line and length, as well as in a defensive mode. They knew that when one of them was struggling against a particular bowler, or didn't look as though he knew where the next run was coming from, both of them would be alert for the short single. The striker would look to drop the ball at his feet or push it into a gap between the infielders and the pair would scamper through for a sharp single to relieve the pressure. The pair of them made that an artform, so it was no surprise that Simpson was so keen to instil it into the Australian team when he took over. He knew that one-day batting was not about big hits or big misses — it was a controlled assault that relied on regular pushes and nudges to keep the scoreboard ticking as much as it did on flamboyant strokes that bounced once or twice before smashing into the fence.

It was all about improvising to keep the score moving. The famous line attributed to Simpson was that: 'The team that scores the most ones will win the match.' Now I don't know if that is quite the case, particularly on the flint-hard outfields of the subcontinent and the West Indies where, once the ball gets through the infield, it will invariably race away for four. But I would certainly agree that the team that managed to score at a run a ball would be almost unbeatable.

I have heard Simpson explain his philosophy of batting like this: you weigh up every ball on its merits and see if you can hit it for four. If not four, then three. Or two.

One-day cricket demands innovative strokeplay, but there is still a big role for orthodox shots such as this sweep.

Or if you can't score two, can you get a single? Every ball has the potential to be scored off but it is only by transforming that potential into action that you can build a winning score.

That doesn't mean that you should be looking to smash a four off every ball, or even a single off every ball. You must be alert to the potential of every delivery and if you are capable of harvesting that potential more often than the opposition, it is likely you will build a higher score. After all, that is what the game is all about.

# Your Natural Game

But how do you get that run a ball? Play your natural game. This is what Steve Waugh said to me as I walked out to open for the first time in a one-day match, and it is the primary piece of advice I give to any young player who asks me how they should improve their game. You can't play like Mark Waugh if you are David Boon, so you shouldn't try to.

Batsmen, in particular, need to work out their strengths and play to them. If you are a good front-foot player, you should be looking to reap the benefits when the ball is full. Think: 'If I get a half-volley first ball, I won't try to pat it back – I will try to put it through the covers for four.'

The same applies if you are strong against the short ball and you get a loose one early that deserves to be put away. Or if your style is to accumulate runs, you need to work hard on that part of your game so that you can make the most of it. There is no point trying to hit good-length balls back over the bowler's head when you are best suited to gliding the ball away or nudging it into the gaps.

But for all that, one-day cricket demands that its players are versatile and able to adapt to different

27

conditions. Players must be able to improvise. Of course, playing aggressively or your natural game can sometimes lead to your dismissal. But that's one-day cricket. It is about taking risks.

Greg Norman has a saying that translates well to the one-day cricket field. He says his golden rule of golf is: 'Believe in yourself.' I agree with that 100 per cent but I would add this saying as well: know your game. If you can analyse your game objectively and you are prepared to work hard to maintain your strengths and improve your weaknesses, you will be able to make an impact in one-day cricket.

Many players have a set plan, or play their innings over and over in their mind before they actually get to the crease. For me, this is a waste of time and energy. Although you might have a target to chase, or have some idea of the total the team thinks it should score, you have to be prepared to adjust to the conditions – whether it is the pitch, the bowling, or the state of the game – and play accordingly.

I don't have a structured game plan other than to watch the ball closely. The old coaching manual line to treat every ball on its merits certainly still applies, but you must remember that the one-day game doesn't allow you to miss opportunities to score. One-day cricket does not allow you to pat back ball after ball, or over after over, just because the bowling is tight and it is difficult to score. Doing that simply builds pressure on yourself, the batsman at the other end, and the rest of your teammates.

But you will need to take the game up to the opposition no matter how you play. Think of the ways you can break up the field. Work on your running. If you are playing a series of defensive shots, be aware that you can drop your hands as you play the ball so that it rolls away without any power and you have time to run through for a single. Be versatile and creative. Even so, you should try to play your natural

28

game as much as you can while seeking ways to disrupt the bowlers and fieldsmen. That's where the Simpson plan is so effective. We will look at that in more detail shortly.

When I walk to the crease, I think to myself that if the first ball is a half-volley, my natural instinct is to go after it and play a cover drive. That means I am preparing to bat with positive thoughts in my mind and I am alert to the fact that if the ball is in the right spot, I will have a go at it.

I was thinking this when I walked to the crease at Sutherlands Park, the home of Perth grade cricket club, Gosnells, to open in a one-day match for Perth in October 1997. About three hours later, I walked into the pavilion for a cup of tea after knocking up 252, a WACA one-day record, which included 28 fours and 8 sixes. It only took 157 balls, too.

I didn't have anything other than my normal thoughts as I walked out that day – watch the ball, be aggressive, play your natural game. But early in the innings, I realised that the pitch was a beauty for batting, and more importantly perhaps, the bowling line-up contained nothing but medium-pacers. Gosnells had no quick bowlers and no spinners, so their variety was limited. I thought that if I could get settled in and get a feel for the pace and bounce of the pitch, I could really take on the bowling. There weren't going to be any surprises because all the bowlers were so similar. And by taking on the bowlers, I meant to be aggressive, take calculated risks and back my own ability. As it turned out, everything fell into place for me.

The same thing happened when I scored 154 against Sri Lanka in Melbourne in January 1999. I went to the middle thinking my usual thoughts about being aggressive and watching the ball. This time, though, I was lucky to get off the mark, let alone go on to set an MCG record. If Pramodya Wickremesinghe, the big Sri Lankan opening bowler, had been able to throw straight, I would have finished with a duck after a near-disastrous mix-up with Mark Waugh. Soon after that though, I got a few runs under my belt and then I struck a purple patch when every shot I played seemed to hit the middle of the bat and race to the boundary. After getting off to that flyer, it was just a matter of batting normally and seeing off the overs. The pitch was good and the outfield lightning-fast. Just like that day at Gosnells, the risks all seemed to pay off.

Batsmen can afford to be more cautious in the longer game, whether it is a Test match or a grade match on the weekend. You can structure an innings in these matches. You know you can bat for survival for half an hour or more and then start to slowly knock them around. That's where the coaching manual advice comes in handy – build your innings, take every ball on its merits and when you have your eye in and are starting to hit it well, start to be more aggressive and get on top of the bowling.

You can't be that rigid in one-day cricket, particularly if you bat in the middle or lower order where you don't have the luxury of playing yourself in. Instead, you have to be ready to capitalise from ball one. It might take ten to 15 balls to get off the mark but you also have to be ready to hit a boundary first ball if it is on offer.

# Hitting in the Air

'Slogger' – how many times have you heard this critical word applied to batsmen in one-day cricket? Yet slogging plays only a small part in successful one-day batting. Scoring runs consistently in the one-day game is much more likely to be the result of good technique, good shot selection and good application of what Dean Jones calls 'crease management'.

Except for the last few overs of an innings in which batsmen have to scramble for as many runs as they can get, it is rare for a batsman to slog rather than play proper cricket shots. Astute judges have recognised this, including the most well-credentialled of all. Writing in 1986 in *Wisden*, the bible of cricket, Sir Donald Bradman had this to say of one-day batting:

> *Many cricket enthusiasts claim that the one day game has brought in its wake a decline in batting technique. This may have some validity but it is not necessarily true. People get confused between a normal mode of play and the essential improvisation needed to circumvent defensive fields. Vivian Richards and Clive Lloyd are marvellous examples of batsmen capable of coping quite adequately with both types of cricket without sacrificing any basic soundness of technique. The main difference in their one day attitude has been a willingness to take the risk of lofting the ball over fieldsmen's heads.*

There is a difference between slogging, which is throwing the bat at everything in a haphazard manner, and controlled aggressive hitting such as that demonstrated by the Sri Lankan powerhouse Sanath Jayasuriya, or the Indian genius Sachin Tendulkar. Jayasuriya and his mate Romesh Kaluwitharana, who make up one of the most attacking opening combinations since Gordon Greenidge and Desmond Haynes intimidated opening bowlers in the 1980s, play to a strict game plan.

They do hit in the air but, as Bradman recognised, playing lofted shots rather than keeping the ball along the ground is not 'slogging'. If you watch Sanath Jayasuriya closely, you will see that he has already worked out the areas of the field to which he can most effectively hit the ball and will play to that plan.

31

AN ATTACKING LOFTED SWEEP FORWARD OF SQUARE LEG. KEEPING YOUR HEAD DOWN AND WATCHING THE BALL ONTO THE BAT WILL ENSURE THIS SHOT BRINGS GOOD REWARDS.

Jayasuriya has a superb eye and is a gifted player capable of setting off fireworks other batsmen can only dream about. More importantly, he is a player with a solid technique who sticks to the basics and applies them in spectacular fashion. He did it in Perth in early 1999 when he hit Adam Dale out of the attack with an onslaught that brought him 34 runs in just four overs. Yet none of the shots he used to pulverise the previously miserly Dale were slogs. Rather, they were the result of clean striking through the line that sent the ball straight back the way it came – except at about four times the speed and five times the elevation.

It was scintillating stuff, though I don't know if Dale would agree.

**Sanath Jayasuriya**
Born 30/6/69
188 matches 180 innings 8 not out 4923 runs
151★ highest score 28.62 average 7x100 31x50

The real genius of Jayasuriya is not that he plays better shots than other batsman, but that he plays them earlier, harder and more often than most. If the ball is short, even by a centimetre or two, he will slash it over point or square leg. If it is a good length or full, he will swing the ball over mid-on or mid-off. He still bats in the traditional 'V' – the arc between those two straight positions – but at a tempo matched by few players. If that hittable ball comes on the first delivery of the day, so much the better. It means he can get on the scoreboard immediately and get on with the job. Equally though, if the ball is a good one and Jayasuriya can't put it away, he will demonstrate a copybook defensive technique.

It is no coincidence that the best one-day players are usually also superb Test batsmen. Great batsmen will

33

adapt to any conditions or any style of play required. Jayasuriya has a Test triple-century to his credit, and he would never have scored that if he was simply a slogger without the solid foundation of a good technique and temperament. So, too, the best players in other countries. Brian Lara and Sachin Tendulkar, the best one-day batsmen in the West Indies and India, respectively, are also magnificent players in the longer game.

Pakistan's solid opener Saeed Anwar, who holds the one-day record score of 194, is great at both forms of the game. South African Gary Kirsten has a top score of 188 not out in one-dayers, along with seven other tons to go with his 10 Test centuries. He's no slogger – he's a fine aggressive batsman with the ability to adjust his game to the conditions.

And then there's my opening partner, Mark Waugh. His great skill and versatility have enabled him to stamp a mark of quality on both forms of the game.

# Training

The perfect place to analyse and improve your own game is at training. It is crucial that you train just like you play. The old saying urges you to practise as you play and the modern one takes it a step further.

'Practice makes perfect and perfect practice makes for a better cricketer' should be engraved on the gear bag of every young player. Australian and WA players take that motto literally when we prepare for a one-day match. Not only do we try to train with great intensity to mirror what will happen in a match, but we do everything as though we are already in the game.

Away go the white uniforms and out comes the coloured gear. There isn't a red ball in sight because the fast bowlers are using new white balls. The batsmen put on their coloured pads and hit white balls, and the fieldsmen catch and chase white balls. The lights come on, too, so we can get a feel for the ground and conditions in artificial light.

From the earliest age, coaches advise players to treat net sessions just as they would a real innings in the middle. If the ball is wide, let it go. If it is on the stumps, get behind it and push it back. Start to get a feel for the pitch and light, get your feet moving then begin to play a few shots and work at building your innings. It is no different if you are preparing for a one-day match, except that you have to be ready to respond from the first ball. If you get a half-volley first ball in a one-day match, you have to put it away through the covers. It's the same in the nets. Have in your mind that you are required to score from the first ball of the day and that is the way you should think as you walk in to start your 15- or 20-minute net session. If the ball is there to be hit, hit it.

If it is not in the right spot for a big shot, drop it at your feet or work it towards the area where you know there will be a gap. Don't just think that the ball is a good one and can't be scored off. You may face deliveries in a match that are genuinely unplayable or can't be pushed for a single, but work at squeezing the most you can out of the potential of every ball. This requires mental discipline and the ability to focus on every ball, even with the distractions that seem part of every net session.

Take a leaf out of Michael Bevan's book. Bevan is arguably the best one-day batsman in the world because of his uncanny ability to score at nearly a run a ball, no matter what conditions he faces. His record is astounding. He has 3822 runs at an average of almost 60 with a career strike rate of 79 runs per 100 balls, yet his achievements have not arisen by accident. He works on his game as hard as any player and you can see the benefits.

When Bevan walks into the nets to face the bowling, he does several things. First, he summons a picture in his mind of where the field would be set. Then he weighs up the bowling attack and works out where he can play shots to score runs. Then, exactly as he does when he walks to the middle, he works on placing the ball into the gaps.

He improvises by whipping good-length balls from outside off-stump towards square leg. Or he steps outside leg-stump to squirt the ball through the covers. He is always trying to stay one step ahead of the bowlers and forcing them to surrender their own game plan. There is nothing accidental about it – Bevan has a plan and, knowing he has the right tools to carry it out, works methodically towards his aim of not getting out and hitting every ball into a gap.

Practise all the things you are going to do in the game. Earlier, I referred to the need to know your game. One way of stretching yourself, both to discover your limits and to go beyond them, is to try things in the nets.

Try big shots back over the bowler's head. Try charging him to see if you can hit the ball while you are on the move. These suggestions might seem unorthodox, especially when you see coaches and net captains annoyed at what they deem to be rash or undisciplined shots. Hitting the ball in the air is a skill, just like keeping it on the ground. The player who has practised it well will find himself better able to play it when needed. There is no point walking to the middle when the team needs a boundary off the last ball to win a match and realising that you have never hit a bowler back over his head before. The nets are the ideal place to find out things about your individual skill and talent.

Perhaps you are better suited to playing shots that might not clear the boundary but are valuable in that they can be chipped into open space to allow you to run two or three. Ian Healy is a fine example of a player who is not a known long hitter of the ball. By thoroughly knowing his own game, he is able to score at a run a ball by regularly knocking it short of the deep fieldsmen. How many times have you seen him play a lofted drive that drops two-thirds of the way to the boundary at midwicket and allows him to pick up two?

Other players might fancy themselves to hit it over the deep fieldsmen, but that comes at a risk. Others will not play a lofted shot at all but will attempt to run it away for a single. Heals comes between the two types of players because he has assessed his game – he has realised he can play the chip shot well and worked hard to hone that skill.

**Ian Healy**
Born 3/4/64
168 matches 120 innings 36 not out 1764 runs
56 highest score 21.00 average 4x50

A golfer practises with all his clubs – from a putter to a sand wedge to a driver – because he wants his swing to be perfectly grooved for the shots he needs to play with them. So, too, should a batsman practise all his shots.

Jayasuriya doesn't just walk to the middle and start hitting balls into the stratosphere by accident – he has worked on hitting short balls hard and high over point or square leg and hitting full balls back over the bowler, so when the right ball is bowled in a match, he is ready and able to give it the treatment.

Darren Lehmann used the nets in the summer of 1997/98 to overcome a problem we were having with South African off-spinner, Pat Symcox. The veteran offie is one of the blokes you both love and hate to play against. He is a bubbly and passionate character, so there is always likely to be action on the cricket field when he's on it. At a match in Sydney in which a spectator threw a barbecued chicken at Pat as he stood at fine leg, he responded by quipping: 'That was the most foul thing I have ever seen on a cricket field.'

Symcox is an awkward customer to face because of his height and ability to get the ball to bounce from a good length. He actually opened the bowling in Perth during 1997/98 and made a good fist of it by picking up 2–33 from his ten overs. We had four left-handers in the top seven in that match – Jim Maher, Lehmann, Bevan and myself – and Symcox was able to exploit the advantage he had gained during the series. He had started to get the wood on a few of us by coming around the wicket and spearing the ball in at the legs.

### Pat Symcox
Born 14/4/60
68 matches 588.4 overs 2360 runs 64 wickets 35.77 average
53.81 strike rate 4–28 best bowling 4.11 runs per over

He would get bounce from a full length because of his height and, with his great accuracy, he was able to tie us down and make it difficult for us to get him away. It was a classic example of a bowler working out a strategy and putting it into practice. But Darren Lehmann helped us overcome the Symcox problem.

Instead of batting with a normal guard on middle- or middle- and leg-stumps, Lehmann took guard on or even outside leg-stump. He then backed away even more when Symcox bowled and then swatted him through the off-side. It was a risky ploy, but Lehmann got away with it because he had thought it out, practising it again and again in the nets until he was sure it would be effective. When it came time to try it in the match, he was confident it would work. The proof was in the pudding in the first final because he finished up with a solid 31 while Symcox gave up 56 off his ten overs without taking a wicket.

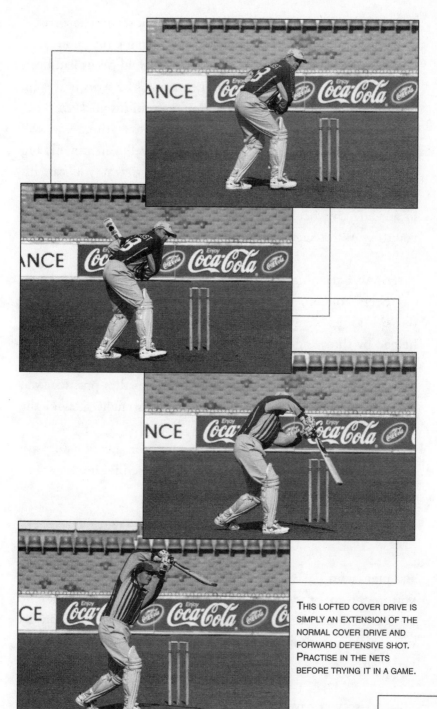

This lofted cover drive is simply an extension of the normal cover drive and forward defensive shot. Practise in the nets before trying it in a game.

Ironically, Symcox only took the one wicket in the finals – Lehmann himself, who was caught at point trying the same tactic in the third match in Sydney. But Symcox's hold on us had been broken. It was a small battle but Lehmann had won it despite Symcox finishing with the consolation prize of his wicket.

It shows how important it is to practise everything you will do in the match. If you are unsure how well you can hit big shots, ask someone to throw balls to you so that you can hit with confidence. Even slow, looping throws from ten metres or so are effective because they get your feet moving and enable you to work on keeping your head down and to hit through the ball.

My WA teammate Justin Langer is one player I know who has been concerned about getting down the wicket to hit through lofted straight drives. After working hard on the ploy – helped by throwing-machine Tom Moody – he was able to feel more comfortable about pulling out the shot if the situation required. This, too, showed how valuable the practice was because he pulled out a couple of superb straight sixes in the West Indies in 1999.

It gets easier and you feel more comfortable if you have practised the things you will need to do in the middle.

# Openers

Batsmen who get to open in one-day cricket are lucky. Now you might query my thinking here, particularly as openers tend to face the meanest, quickest and liveliest bowlers around, but let me explain a few things in favour of the players who take on the new ball.

First, you have the opportunity to bat for 50 overs so you have more of a chance to get a big score, as well as enjoy the luxury of having a few overs to analyse the conditions and get your eye in. A batsman who comes in with five overs to go can't do that – he has to get the scoreboard ticking immediately.

Just over 450 centuries have been scored in international one-dayers up until the end of the 1999 World Cup, with slightly more than half coming from openers. Sachin Tendulkar (23 centuries), Desmond Haynes (17), Saeed Anwar (17), Mark Waugh (12), Gordon Greenidge (11) and Geoff Marsh (9) are all openers with multiples tons to their credit.

Compare that with brilliant and experienced one-day batsmen like Allan Border (3), Steve Waugh (2) and Clive Lloyd (1), and you can see how hard it is to score hundreds coming in lower down the order.

Then there is the situation with those big, hairy quicks. Unfortunately for them, the rules of one-day cricket are weighted towards us batsmen. And don't we love it. They can't bowl too wide or they will be penalised. They can't bowl too short or they will be penalised again. They can't afford to have too many fieldsmen in catching positions because we are going to play shots, and they have to keep the runs down. But they are only allowed two fieldsmen outside the circle for the first 15 overs, so get the ball through the ring and there's a good chance there will be a four on the board.

And there's the ball to take into account. Of course it will swing around or cut off the pitch while it's new, but with pitches designed to assist the batsmen rather than bowlers, and the hardness of the Kookaburra helping it race away from the bat, there is still great return for playing shots at the top of the order.

That is why so many teams elevate their best strokeplayers to an opening berth. Mark Waugh in Australia, Tendulkar for India, even Ian Botham back in the World Cup in

Australia and New Zealand in 1992 have all been promoted because they are orthodox batsmen with good techniques who can defend against the moving ball if necessary. But their natural attacking games mean they will get plenty of runs if they can bat for a reasonable number of overs at the start of the innings. This is a prime example of the one-day game evolving as more matches are played and strategies are analysed.

**Sachin Tendulkar**
Born 24/4/73
222 matches 215 innings 21 not out 8310 runs
143 highest score 42.83 average 23x100 44x50

One of the best one-day innings of the modern era was played by Sachin Tendulkar in his hometown of Bombay during the 1996 World Cup match against Australia. Our attack was very strong – with key strikers Glenn McGrath, Damien Fleming and Shane Warne – and we were confident of defending the total of 258.

Tendulkar was the key to India's hopes, which started to look pretty threadbare when they lost two wickets to Fleming in the first few overs. But Tendulkar was unruffled. He batted patiently for 30 minutes or so, assessing the pace and bounce of the pitch, analysing whether the bowlers were getting any movement and testing how the newly installed lights affected his vision. He pushed a single or two, played two or three forceful shots, but did little more than consider each delivery on its merits. Suddenly, he launched an attack on McGrath that was breathtaking in its ferocity. Four after four was dispatched as Tendulkar thrashed McGrath for 27 from two overs and drove the paceman out of the attack.

Fortunately for Australia, there was no fairytale ending for India. They fell 16 runs short as Fleming cleaned up the middle order. Tendulkar was eventually dismissed for 90 off 88 balls – stumped by Ian Healy off a Mark Waugh wide – but not before playing one of the most astounding innings of his career.

It was a superb demonstration of a batsman who played everything on its merits in traditional fashion before deciding the time had come for him to impose his mark on the game. Tendulkar didn't have a set plan that day, he just batted as the conditions required and then put his foot on the accelerator pedal when the time was right. But he had the luxury that we openers have – the opportunity to take a few overs to get set. As an opener, this is an advantage, but there is also an added pressure. If you invest early overs as a means of getting your eye in, you have to pay a dividend by batting a considerable amount of time and earning plenty of runs.

The role of openers has changed somewhat over the past decade or so as teams try different strategies to build a winning score. In the early days of one-day cricket, the approach was similar to Test matches – a solid foundation would be laid in the first 15 or 20 overs to ensure wickets were in hand later on when the team would try to cash in at the happy hour at the end of the innings.

Australia used that strategy for many years by employing solid openers like Geoff Marsh and David Boon whose job it was to bat through the innings. Their task was to turn the strike over but to ensure they were there at the end. Marsh, in particular, was brilliant at this patient approach. He would absorb the good bowling to prevent a rush of wickets, but farm the strike to the more aggressive strokeplayers at the other end who would hit out to build a big score. But Marsh was no stodge. If he was able to bat through to 45-plus overs, he would invariably have 100 on the board and would be capable of some pretty big hitting in the last few overs.

At Chandigarh in the 1987 World Cup match against New Zealand, Marsh demonstrated his clean hitting by smashing 2 sixes in the last over as he finished with 126 not out. I don't think Malcolm Marshall, the great West Indian fast bowler, will ever forget being drop-kicked over the long-on fence – that was the fence around Barbados's Kensington Oval, not the fence around the playing area – as Swampy carved his way to 113 in 1991.

**Geoff Marsh**
Born 31/12/58
117 matches 115 innings 6 not out 4357 runs
126* highest score 39.97 average 9x100 22x50

Marsh was our coach for several years, but we have made a slight shift away from that strategy, particularly on the subcontinent where the conditions make it is easier to score earlier in the innings. Playing in Australia is a little different because the extra bounce and bigger grounds make it harder for the big hitters. There is not such an imperative to get runs early, though, because the ball will retain its hardness throughout the innings.

We have found that a more conservative style of one-day cricket is more successful in Australia. It involves building a foundation to start, then capitalising on the good start in the middle before coming home in a rush. In India and Pakistan, where the ball starts to resemble an old tennis ball after 30 or 40 overs, it is very difficult to get any great power on it in the last part of the innings. The ball loses chunks of leather, it becomes quite soft and seems to absorb any energy applied to it with the bat. Playing more shots early is not just a chance to build a solid foundation, it must also be used to put up a few walls and the odd roof as well.

Even so, the Australian one-day team now requires both openers to be aggressive. We often use middle-order batsmen like Michael Bevan or Steve Waugh to guide the team through to the 50-over mark. This is the result of a slight shift in one-day thinking brought about first by the West Indian master blasters and then, more recently, by the Sri Lankan method of attacking early and consolidating later.

As I described earlier, the ball is harder early in the innings and with the field up inside the ring, there are often more opportunities to score in the early overs. Most one-day teams now try to score at four or five an over in the first 15, or even more if the conditions allow, rather than the solid two or three an over of past days.

With the faster run rate comes the increased chance of losing wickets, which is a factor that must be considered in the team's planning. Many teams, particularly those with strong middle orders or those such as South Africa with an abundance of all-rounders low in the line-up, would be prepared to sacrifice a wicket or two early if it means they can get 90 or 100 on the board.

From that good start, you can then survey the situation and consolidate or hit out even more. Many teams do that nowadays, from Western Australia which uses Ryan Campbell as an attacking and clean-hitting opener with a licence to go after the bowling, to many English county teams that employ at least one hitter in the top order in the 40- and 50-over competitions. It means openers have to be prepared to clear the infield, with the associated element of risk, but explains why Jayasuriya and Tendulkar are such dangerous one-day players.

Remember to play your natural game, though, and be alert to the conditions. I fell into a trap while playing against India and Zimbabwe at the Pepsi Cup tournament in April 1998. I was trying to launch at every ball bowled to me, rather than belting the ones that deserved to be hit and simply pushing around the rest. It was a mistake, as my results indicated pretty clearly.

After scoring 61 against India at Cochin, in a game that was played in the hottest and most uncomfortable conditions of my career – I felt like I was wading between the wickets because of the sweat that had soaked my socks and turned my boots into squelching blobs of boiling treacle – I managed just 12, 11, 1 and 1. It was a hard but valuable lesson. Instead of reaping the rewards of playing a lengthy innings on small grounds with lightning-fast outfields, I tried to hit too hard too early and ended up sitting in the pavilion grinding my teeth.

Now, I don't envy my middle-order teammates for having the opportunity to get a good score, but I was annoyed at myself for not carrying out my own job. By the time we had moved to Sharjah later that month, and changed drinking habits seeing that it was now the Coca-Cola Cup we were playing for, I had worked on my approach and managed to score 57 against New Zealand, plus 45 against India in the final, which they ended up winning comfortably by six wickets. That was a good reminder that you still have to temper aggression with smart thinking, and that you don't have to hit over the top to be effective.

As he showed in that World Cup match in Bombay, Tendulkar rarely hits over the top in the early part of his innings. He plays traditional shots – cut shots if the ball is short, pushes and nudges off his pads if it is a good line and length – before having a go later. Even then, he doesn't always go through with his shot if he feels it is not the best option. If Tendulkar gets into position to smash one over cover and the ball is not in the right spot, he will often pull out of the shot and push it back to the bowler.

Mind you, often it seems he has almost been beaten, then he suddenly changes his angle and smashes the ball over midwicket rather than cover. But then he's a genius and he can do things that plenty of coaches have not even heard of, let alone put in their manual!

Work out the best approach for your own game. It is no good trying to smash opening bowlers over point like Jayasuriya does if you feel uncomfortable playing that sort of shot. Many young players, in particular, will not have the strength to play big shots like that which tend to be delivered with an enormous amount of oomph. You need to be aggressive, but know that it is not going to work every time. It is important to weigh up the conditions and decide if you want to try to get 50 off 40 balls or 100 off 80 and risk losing a few wickets, or playing more conservatively. Often it depends on whether you have a solid enough team around that can counter the early dismissals.

One-day teams are tending to play more all-rounders which means they can be more aggressive at the top of the order. The team that has batting depth to No. 8 or No. 9 can cover for the loss of an early wicket. People have criticised Ryan Campbell for trying to go after the bowling from the first ball but that is a tactic the WA team adopts because we are confident that we have plenty of other batsmen who can fire if Ryan doesn't. But if Ryan comes off and scores 60 in 50 balls, for example, we are in a very strong position.

**Ryan Campbell**
Born 14/2/72
(for Westen Australia) 24 matches 24 innings 0 not out 530 runs 72 highest score 22.08 average 4x50

# No. 3

Pilot, architect, engineer – the player batting at No. 3 has to be all these and more. No. 3 is the position traditionally occupied by the best player in the team, the player most capable of controlling the destiny of the innings. No wonder the biggest names in one-day cricket and first-drop batsmen are so often one and the same. Viv Richards, Dean Jones, Javed Miandad, Brian Lara, Zaheer Abbas, Aravinda De Silva – they are all undisputed champions of the game; players who dominated attacks from their position in the engine-room of their team's innings. Imagine how daunting it must have been for bowlers who faced the West Indies in the mid 1980s. Any joy brought by the early dismissal of Desmond Haynes or Gordon Greenidge would have quickly vanished when the gate opened and out strolled the Master Blaster, Viv Richards, 3-pound bat in his hand and maroon cap perched majestically on his head, with an air of invincibility and absolute certainty that he was about to wreak havoc.

**Viv Richards**
Born 7/3/52
187 matches 167 innings 24 not out 6721 runs
189* highest score 47.00 average 11x100 45x50

That he certainly did in Melbourne in December 1979 when he belted Australia from deep midwicket to deep cover and all points in between as he slammed 153 not out. That remained the MCG record for 19 years until I played a few shots of my own against Sri Lanka and ended up beating it by 1 run.

The same mixture of relief and anguish brought by the end of Greenidge or Haynes would have been matched by the teams that managed to chip out David Boon or Geoff Marsh in the 1980s, only to have the hyperactive Dean Jones come to the crease and start the aggressive running and innovative strokeplay that were his hallmarks.

Players at No. 3 are invariably aggressive – like Richards and Jones – but they must also be technically adept. After all, they could start their innings on the second ball of the match or the second-last ball. Some days the No. 3 will be in after quite a few overs have been bowled and he will have to play the traditional middle-order role of keeping the runs flowing and the pressure on the fielding team. Other days he will be required to play as a virtual opener, particularly if the bowlers are on top and there is plenty of life in the pitch.

The No. 3 has to be versatile – the hallmark of one-day cricket, of course – and ready to respond to any situation.

Australia has done well with Ricky Ponting batting at three for the past couple of seasons. He has a good defence, which makes him ideal to combat strong early bowling. But he is aggressive and capable of scoring quickly, so his mere presence puts pressure on the fielding team.

Ricky is one of my favourite players for another reason. In the five centuries I have scored for Australia, who has been standing at the non-striker's end each time I have brought up the ton? That's right. None other than R.T. Ponting, the lively lad from Launceston, who seems to have the uncanny knack of bringing out the best in my batting. Perhaps it's the fact that he is so quick on his feet and able to provide so much trouble for the bowlers that it takes a bit of heat off me. Or maybe it's because he doesn't let me get into a comfort zone and constantly chips at me to concentrate and work the ball around.

**Ricky Ponting**
Born 19/12/74
88 matches 88 innings 10 not out 3022 runs
145 highest score 38.74 average 5x100 15x50

The confidence that Ricky has in his own ability is something that rubs off onto his partner when they are batting together. He has always backed his ability to win more contests against bowlers than he loses. It is not an uncommon sight to see Punter stride out to take on the quickest bowlers in the world with only the green and gold cap of Australia on his head. Bowlers often take to that like a bull to a red cape and start to bowl shorter to the batsman to give him a scare. But Ricky knows he is one of the best exponents of the hook shot in the game, so he is not afraid to issue a challenge to the bowler.

Now wearing a helmet is something I thoroughly recommend at all levels of cricket but, as you can see, a classy player like Ponting has the confidence in his own ability to thrive in most situations. And, again, this confidence will often rub off on the batsman lucky enough to be in the middle with him.

Ricky and I certainly combined well in Lahore in October 1998 when we both got tons against Pakistan, though I was disappointed to not be able to return the favour by being at the non-striker's end when Ricky got to three figures.

Even so, he knows the right thing to say when a milestone has been missed. He and I put on 74 for the second wicket in Sydney in January 1999 as we chased the target of 260 set by Sri Lanka. It seemed a pretty easy task after Mark Waugh and I had opened with 151 in quick time, and with every ball hitting the middle of Ricky's blade, there was a certain amount of inevitability about our batting. Unfortunately for me, I tried to get it over with too quickly and ended up holing out to Marvan Atapattu off Chaminda Vaas for 131 when we needed just 35 with plenty of time to spare.

Not only had I let the team down by getting out when the job was still unfinished, but Ricky would not let me forget that I had failed to break the Australian one-day record he shared with Dean Jones. Mind you, he confided to me later that if I had got too close, he would

50

have run me out. Now I think he was joking, but you never know … That record was 145 and I had a golden opportunity to go past it that day.

I didn't forget Ricky's jibe, however, and didn't miss the chance I had three weeks later. This time it was at the MCG, but it was still Sri Lanka and still the cheeky Tasmanian standing at the other end when I cracked the ton. But this time, I was determined to silence him and finally did so when I moved through the 140s and ended up on 154. Ricky had been dismissed by the time I reached the record, but even though I had taken it from him, he was quick to congratulate me after I got back into the dressing rooms. He also said he was excited because he now had a record to chase and was sure he would knock it off one day soon. Good luck Punter, and *you* had better watch your running, too!

State teams around Australia provide interesting theories about who should bat at No. 3. In Western Australia, Damien Martyn has held down the No. 3 position for the past few years and has done tremendously well in the role. He is a natural strokeplayer able to dominate an attack on his day. But he also has a solid technique and is not out of his depth against good bowling on a lively deck. He has certainly carried his form through to international level and has slotted well into the job of batting first wicket down in several one-dayers for Australia in the absence of Ponting. Martyn also showed his versatility by slotting in at No. 5 and No. 6 for Australia last season. Justin Langer, the Test No. 3, has also batted there for the Warriors, but he tends to open or bat at No. 4 when Marto is playing.

Langer is a patient batsman who is more in the Geoff Marsh mould, but he is quite capable of playing the big shots required as well as turning the strike over. They are two different types of player, but both are very effective.

51

## Playing for WA in domestic one-day matches

| | | | | | | | | |
|---|---|---|---|---|---|---|---|---|
| **Damien Martyn** | 42m | 40i | 7no | 1540r | 140hs | 46.66ave | 2x100 | 12x50 |
| **Justin Langer** | 38m | 37i | 4no | 1263r | 96hs | 38.27ave | 0x100 | 12x50 |

New South Wales has had quite a dilemma with their batting line-up in recent seasons – they have had to juggle some tremendous players into the places they can be most effective. With openers Mark Taylor and Michael Slater being such an effective combination, there has been no need to employ Mark Waugh in that post despite the great job he has done for Australia over the past few years.

Interestingly, both Mark and I open in the one-dayers for Australia but neither of us open for our state teams in Sheffield Shield or Mercantile Mutual matches. Even so, we seem to work pretty well together. I must admit there are times I would like to walk out to the middle of the WACA to face the new ball in domestic games.

Mark Waugh bats at No. 4 for New South Wales, allowing his national captain and twin brother to slot into No. 3. And if that first four isn't daunting enough for opposition attacks, then comes Michael Bevan at No. 5 to continue the torment. He also bats at No. 3 when the Waughs are absent and has proved as much a master in that position as he has done further down the list.

No matter who gets the nod at three, the same rule of thumb applies – whoever bats there is likely to be a tremendous player and is capable of scoring quickly or seeing off a good spell of bowling, depending on the circumstances. Unless there is a good reason for batting your best player somewhere else, perhaps by using him as an opener as India does with Sachin Tendulkar, it pays to have him at No. 3. No matter how the game has changed over the years, that is one factor that has remained constant.

# Middle Order

There are mixed blessings in being a player who bats from No. 4 through to No. 7, yet the success of a one-day team invariably depends on the performance of one or more batsmen in this part of the line-up.

Just like the No. 3, some days will require the batsmen to come in with the team in trouble with two or three wickets down and few runs on the board. Other days, the batsmen sit in the pavilion for over after over as the top order flays the bowling, only to be thrown in with a few balls to go and the difficult task of maintaining the momentum. It is a tough job and this is reflected in the fact that few middle-order batsmen manage to average much more than 30 or so in one-day matches – apart from Michael Bevan. More on him later.

And that's not because they are poor batsmen. Allan Border, David Gower and Steve Waugh have been sensational one-day players, but they all average in the low 30s which reflects the risks they have had to take to boost their team's total. More often than not, these players have to swing the bat at the end of the innings and end up sacrificing their wickets for the sake of the team.

Middle-order positions are no place for the faint-hearted, nor for those players who like to keep a close eye on the averages and don't mind being left at the non-striker's end with the red ink at the end of 50 overs. It is the place for good strokeplayers and those batsmen capable of turning the strike over and taking plenty of quick singles.

Steve Waugh is an interesting example of a player who performs in different ways depending on the job he has to do. When he plays Test matches, Waugh is as solid as a block of granite. Bowlers chip away at him for hour

53

after hour without seeming to make the slightest impression on his resolve. He might take 300 balls to get to 100 and just keeps concentrating on removing all risk from his play. If the ball is not there to be hit, he won't try to hit it. Even if it takes five or ten overs before he gets a ball to put away, so be it.

Waugh is very different in one-day matches. He was a flamboyant and daring shotmaker as a young player, who simply decided success at the elite level required him to put away most of the colourful and risky strokes. Even so, the odd cover drive and pull shot reminds Test bowlers that he still has plenty of sting in his tail.

**Steve Waugh**
Born 2/6/65
273 matches 247 innings 48 not out 6306 runs
120* highest score 31.68 average 2x100 37x50

Waugh brings out more of those shots in the one-day arena but, more importantly, tries to get the bat on every ball he faces to enable him to score at a run a ball. How many times have you seen him play the nudge through the leg-side from a good-length ball? It is little more than a defensive shot but he uses that to keep the scoreboard ticking.

He is capable of playing sparkling innings, too, when the team needs it most. No one who saw Waugh take on the might of the South African bowling in the World Cup match at Headingley will ever forget his audacity and breathtaking strokeplay. He came to the crease with the team in dire straits at 3–48 in reply to the Proteas' score of 271 with the weight of his country's expectation on him. If Australia lost, we were out of the tournament.

Waugh would have nothing of that. He built a foundation with solid defence mingled with plenty of quick singles to keep building the score. He then put his foot down to launch an attack when he thought the time was right. He produced drives, pulls and his unorthodox but effective slog-sweep, a shot he has reintroduced in the last year or so, as he ground the bowlers down and forced them to play at his tempo.

Sachin Tendulkar scored a century against us at Sharjah in 1998 that I thought was the best one-day innings I have seen, but Waugh's effort was even more special. Given the calibre of the opposition, the difficult batting conditions, the significance of the tournament and the fact that Australia would drop out of the World Cup if it failed to reach the target, his performance ranks among the very best one-day innings ever played.

It is essential for middle-order batsmen to keep getting bat on ball. It seems obvious that it is impossible to score runs without hitting the ball, yet so many batsmen, particularly in the second half of the innings, do nothing with deliveries that could be pushed or glided for an easy single.

THE ONE-DAY BATSMAN'S STOCK SHOT — THE GLIDE TO THIRD MAN OFF THE BACK AND FRONT FOOT.

BATTING

Defensive shots can be turned into drop-and-run singles. Balls that are off the stumps need to be turned away if they can not be attacked with an orthodox drive or cut. The squirt to third man – the quintessential one-day shot – is regularly played at this time of the innings. It is the equivalent of the bowler's stock ball – a simple angling of the bat to turn the ball through the slips area which is invariably vacant after the first 15 overs. Most batsmen practise this in the nets until it almost becomes second nature.

Coming in late is the toughest time to begin an innings, so it is imperative to learn from every game you play in to become better prepared next time.

Employing pinch-hitters to accelerate the scoring rate is an idea that some captains are keen on and others have no time for. Steve Waugh uses this strategy often, particularly if the openers have got off to a good start – he'll see the benefit in promoting natural hitters like Brendon Julian or Shane Lee to maintain the pressure on the fielding team. This tactic is not always going to work. It's not as important for a strong batting team. But a team that knows the limitations of its batsmen might be keen to gamble on a hitter being a match-winner.

Probably the most famous example of a pinch-hitter changing the tone of a match (as much as pushing the scoring rate along) was the World Cup quarter-final in Madras in 1996 when Australia overhauled the 287 target set by New Zealand. After a solid but careful start that saw Australia reach 2–84 from 20 overs, Mark Taylor sprang a surprise by sending in Shane Warne with a brief to set off some fireworks. That he did, with Warne delighting the 45 000 people at the Chidambaram Stadium as he clobbered two huge sixes in his 24 off 14 balls. Although he was out at 127, the momentum created by the Warne whirlwind fired Australia on, and we simply counted down to the target as Mark Waugh finished the innings off with a marvellous run-a-ball 110.

The tactic didn't work a week later in the final, though, proving that the risks taken in one-day cricket don't always go your way. This time Warne made only 2 off 5 balls after he was sent in with Australia doing reasonably well at 3–152.

One-day cricket demands that its players are versatile and ready to respond, so it is vital that batsmen sitting in the pavilion are ready for the call to pad up. It doesn't happen all the time, but sometimes the captain will decide to promote a batsman – perhaps to get a left-hander in, or to use a player better equipped to combat spin bowlers on a turning pitch.

Therefore, all the team – not just the next batsman due in – should be watching the game and soaking up as much as they can from what is happening in front of them. Do any of the fieldsmen have poor throwing arms and look vulnerable to giving up two runs? Is one bowler looking more dangerous than the rest and might need to be seen off? Is the ball turning? How fast is the outfield? These are all questions worth considering as you wait to bat.

Batsmen already padded up must realise there are times when they might be pushed down the order. This can be a blessing in disguise, because many batsmen play their innings mentally before they get to the middle and find they are exhausted when they finally get there.

But it can also be annoying to someone who is ready to go to find suddenly that the handbrake has been pulled. Greg Blewett found himself in this situation, but it was his hometown Adelaide Oval crowd that seemed the most disappointed with his demotion down the order. It was the second match of the triangular series in 1997/98 and Blewett was listed to bat at No. 3 against New Zealand.

It was my second match as Australia's keeper after I replaced Ian Healy and it came a few days after I had copped a torrid time from the Sydney crowd, unhappy with the selection decision. The Kiwis put on a competitive total of 260, but we were looking good when openers Mark Waugh and Michael DiVenuto took the score to 156 before the dashing Tasmanian was out for a cracking 77. I had been promoted from No. 6 with instructions to keep the runs flowing and was looking forward to the task as I walked to the crease, particularly as the Adelaide crowd gave me an enthusiastic reaction completely different from that in Sydney. 'Beauty,' I thought. 'I've been forgiven for taking Heals's place. I'll play a few shots and perhaps they might come around to my side even more.'

Wrong. I hadn't quite reached the middle when the ground announcer, realising there had been a change in the batting line-up, broadcast the name of the new batsman. The response was immediate. The cheers for the hometown hero were replaced by boos for the West Australian interloper as the 30 000-strong crowd suddenly sounded as though it had doubled in size and intensity. Oh well, that was pretty good motivation and I hopefully answered a few of those Croweater critics by making 29 before being run out.

On the other side of the coin, a flexible batting line-up means players are often required to sit for over after over waiting to bat as a long partnership develops in the middle. This makes it important to be able to relax as you watch. Ponting is very good at this part of his game. He knows he could be in second ball or that he might have to wait for two hours for his chance, yet he always seems to have the same demeanour when he gets to the crease. As he showed when he came in at Sydney after Mark Waugh and I had put on 151, he does not get fazed. The ball hit the middle of his bat from the first ball and he cruised to 43 not out with no problem at all.

Michael Bevan is known as The Finisher and it is not hard to see why. Not only is he the best middle-order batsman one-day cricket has ever seen, it is difficult to comprehend anyone ever being better. In 119 games for Australia, Bevan has averaged just less than than 60 – more than 15 runs and 25 per cent better than any other person to have played at least 20 matches. In the history of the game, this display of dominance is probably only matched by Don Bradman.

Bevan gets his runs at nearly 80 per 100 balls, so he is as fast a scorer as most players. And you can count on one hand those players with a better strike rate who actually bat higher in the order than the Canberra-born left-hander who regularly comes in at No. 6.

Some nitpickers say Bevan's average is boosted by the fact that he is left not out in more than a quarter of his innings. Well, it's not his fault that the opposition can't get him out!

He certainly bats long enough for them to have opportunities to knock him over. Bevan has scored three centuries, another 26 fifties and has only failed to reach double figures 12 times in his 105 innings.

His style of play gives the opposition plenty of chances. How many times have you seen Bevan squirt the ball away behind square leg for what can only possibly be one, only for him to hare back for the second as the fieldsmen are left scrambling to return the ball? He doesn't just do it now and then, either. Ball after ball, over after over, Bevan finds the gaps and creates twos from ones and boundaries from good balls. He continues to help Australia turn scores that would have been respectable into formidable targets, or rescues vulnerable innings and turns them into competitive totals.

There is nothing accidental about Bevan's rise to prominence. He is an intense player and has analysed his game with the same microscopic attention to detail that characterised that great technician, Geoff Boycott. Having determined his own strengths and weaknesses, Bevan

59

continues to work exceptionally hard to hone his skills. Often he gets his runs in ones – in the Mercantile Mutual final against WA in March 1994, he scored 77 with 57 of those runs coming in singles.

He is ice-cool. He bats with soft hands, often letting the ball do the work by just angling the bat on it to run it away through the gaps in the field. Bevo works hard on this at training. He is like lightning between the wickets, but speed alone is not enough to enable a player to do as well as he does. Instead, he concentrates on placement and works to put just enough pace and direction on the ball to get the one or two he is after. Bevan is much like a good snooker player who knows exactly where he wants to leave the cue ball after each shot. While most batsmen simply try to control the direction of their shots, Bevan also manipulates the depth of the ball's journey into the outfield. It is a rare gift, yet it is displayed time and again when Bevan is at the crease.

For all his tremendous rescue missions – including setting up gutsy wins over the West Indies with Stuart Law at Chandigarh in the 1996 World Cup semi-final, doing the same thing with Steve Waugh against South Africa in the 1999 World Cup semi-final at Edgbaston and also at Trinidad just before the 1999 World Cup – Bevan is best remembered for just one shot. That was his tremendous straight drive for four off West Indian off-spinner Roger Harper. It gave Australia a one-wicket victory off the last ball of the New Year's Day match in Sydney in 1996.

Bevan made 78 not out that day as he helped Australia to the required 173 after it had been reeling at 6–38. It also demonstrated one of the secrets of Bevan's continued success. Several times in the past few years, he has been asked to speak to the Australian team about his approach to batting in the last two or three overs. He explains that his strategy is to break the field into zones where he can score boundaries and then decide on one or two shots that he will play to each zone depending on where the ball is. If the ball is not in one of the places where he can hit it for four, he uses Plan B which provides the same approach, but identifies regions where he can score ones.

It might have looked like a lucky shot or a bad ball that Bevan was able to hit perfectly straight for the four to win that match in Sydney, but it was much more than that. He had identified the straight boundary as a potential four-scoring zone. When Harper bowled it full and straight, as most bowlers will try to do in the last few overs, he was ready to respond. There were 40 000 people cheering at the SCG that night, but I wonder how many realised the good planning, dedicated practice and superb execution that went into that one shot.

There is never any panic when Bevan is batting. No matter if he is at 4 off 20 balls, he stays calm and is still likely to finish with 50 off 50 balls. He is unbelievable. His target when he walks to the middle is to bat through to the end of the innings and to finish at a run a ball. In fact, he is just about the best exponent of Bob Simpson's theory that if a team can score at one a ball, it won't lose too many matches.

Perhaps Bevan's greatest attribute is his timing. By that I mean he knows when to start pushing the runs along, not just his ability to hit the ball crisply. His mental approach to his batting is so strong that he will use the early overs to get set if he goes in with the team in trouble, but will turn it on from the first ball if he starts batting towards the end of the innings. Bevan's shot placement and running between wickets makes him an ideal role model for all middle-order batsmen. If you are going to model yourself on a prominent player, you shouldn't go wrong by picking the best in the game.

61

# Tailenders

No. 8 to No. 11 do it tough in one-day cricket, but they often have a vital part to play – on the rare occasion they actually get to bat, that is. The nature of one-day cricket means the tailenders are not always going to be required to show their skills with the willow.

Glenn McGrath, for example, has batted in less than a third of the 99 one-dayers he has played. As he is fond of pointing out, his record includes an 18-month stint during 1995 and 1996 when he was not dismissed. 'They couldn't find a bowler good enough to get me out,' the big quick chortles.

**Glenn McGrath**
Born 2/2/70
99 matches 31 innings 17 not out 52 runs
10 highest score 3.71 average

Mind you, he only went to the crease five times during that period and didn't face a ball in a couple of the innings. He might laugh about it, but McGrath knows he has to hold up an end occasionally while the winning runs are scored so he works hard on getting bat on ball and providing an ally to his partner. All tailenders should be prepared to do the same.

You never know when you might be required to score the winning runs or, as McGrath discovered when he went to the crease at the SCG on New Year's Day in 1996, pass the strike to the player who will score them. McGrath did the right thing on that occasion by staying cool, even with the pressure of walking out with five balls to go and six runs needed. It was a fairytale finish. McGrath played his part by building the tension as he failed to score for two balls, before attracting a wide, then nudging the ball around the corner for a single.

Of course, Michael Bevan then did the rest and became an instant hero, but he would not have had the chance without a solid partner at the other end who did not lose his nerve. Anyway, that's the way Glenn describes it and who am I to argue with him?

The most vital thing for batsmen at the end of an innings is to be able to get the bat on the ball. There will invariably be only four fieldsmen in the ring – and they might be set right back on the line – so it should be reasonably easy to score a single simply by dabbing and running. To their credit, most experienced tailenders will do just that, particularly if there is a good batsman at the other end who will look to score a boundary or two. But don't be afraid to play shots, too – the odd four from a No. 11 could be enough to create a winning score.

# Running Between Wickets

Mark Waugh and I have batted together nearly 50 times since I was sent up to open with him against South Africa in January 1998. In all those innings, only four times has one of us fallen victim to our running between wickets. Unfortunately for Mark, he has been the victim three times. Now, I'm not saying whose fault those dismissals were, though I will clearly take the blame for the first one and suggest that there was brilliant fielding involved in the others. Run-outs are an occupational hazard for batsmen in one-day cricket. They are the price you have to pay sometimes for the aggressive running that is such a characteristic of the game.

But while run-outs are the downside, the benefits of aggressive running between wickets far outweigh them. That is why modern one-day players work so hard on their running and use it as a specific tool to combat the opposition's strengths and exploit its weaknesses.

Good running between wickets not only adds numbers to the scoreboard but, used intelligently, can demoralise a fielding team and force it to change its plan of attack. It is an immediate victory for the batsmen if they can force an opposition captain to make a bowling change or alteration to the field that he would rather not make. And it seems to be a characteristic of bowlers worldwide that while they get angry at having a bad ball hit for four, they become furious if a good ball is nudged away for a quick single. Do it two or three times an over and you have a bowler ready to explode ... and perhaps bowl poorly as he struggles to control his temper. If a batsman can achieve that, he has won a small victory and may be able to go on to set up a winning score.

The technique of good running between wickets provides no surprises to anyone who has read a basic coaching manual – no matter what decade in which it was published. The fundamentals are basically the same in all eras: pick the gaps, rotate the strike and take every opportunity to score. But one-day cricket has enhanced those basics by demanding greater intensity from its exponents. W.G. Grace may well have tried to turn the strike over regularly, but it is not likely that he tried to score a run off every ball he faced. That is what one-day batsmen need to do – particularly in the later stages of the team's innings.

So, batsmen have to be alert and ready to run after every shot, the non-striker has to back up well, almost to the point of being in a trot when the ball is about to be bowled, and both players have to run *hard*. This applies whether you are running hard with the ball in the outfield or running hard with the ball only travelling a few metres from the bat.

Apart from Michael Bevan, and unlike Pakistan batsman Inzamam-ul-Haq, whose comical running has caused him to be run out an astonishing 31 times in one-day matches, Dean Jones is probably the best runner between wickets one-day cricket has ever seen. His impact was immediate the moment he came to the crease. You could tell just by looking at him that he was bursting out of his skin and couldn't wait to tear down the other end and try to get back again. Jones made an artform of turning easy singles into hard-run twos because he was so aggressive. He knew that he would win more often than not if he put pressure on the fieldsmen.

Until Jones came along, many batsman who clipped the ball to a fieldsman on the boundary were happy to just take the single. But Jones wasn't satisfied with one. He knew that he could run the 17 metres between the creases quicker than most fieldsmen could gather and throw the ball 70-odd metres back to the stumps. And if he could run the first run in the time it took for the ball to reach the fieldsman, he knew he could turn and sprint back comfortably by the time it was resting in the keeper's gloves. In a season or two of hard and audacious running, Jones changed the nature of one-day cricket enormously.

There was no great secret to his success. Jones was a fast runner, which obviously helped his cause, but it was his attitude as much as his foot-speed that made him such a frustrating player to defend against. But his technique was also good.

**Dean Jones**
Born 24/3/61
164 matches 161 innings 25 not out 6068 runs
145 highest score 44.62 average 7x100 46x50

Unlike many batsmen, Jones ran in a straight line to the other end so he only had to travel the shortest journey possible. Some batsman don't run straight – they tend to veer to the side and run more in an oval or circle pattern. This means they end up taking a step or two more than they have to.

Those extra steps and split-seconds can be crucial, especially if the batsmen are stretching to make their ground and find they need every centimetre to get home in time. When Jones set off for the first run and got near to the other crease, he would stretch his bat out as far as possible to cut down on the distance he needed to run, ground his bat over the line, then push off like a swimmer doing a tumble turn to give himself as much momentum as possible for the second run.

Sometimes he would be so low that he would put his free hand on the pitch to balance himself. He would come back several metres down the pitch as he assessed the position of the ball, then continue to accelerate to make the run or decide against it if it was going to be too dangerous. Either way, he was ready to go because he had taken as short a time as possible to get to the other end and was coming back as hard as he set off.

However, there is one Jones technique that I would not recommend to other players. That was his trait of turning only on his right knee, which meant he would often turn blind. If he played the ball into the off-side, Jones would always turn for the second run with his back to the ball. If it went to the leg-side, he would turn blind for the third run.

This wasn't the result of bad habits creeping into his game, but rather the legacy of a terrible training injury that required a full reconstruction of his left knee and significantly weakened the joint. Jones hurt the knee when Merv Hughes cannoned into him during a game of fielding soccer in February 1987.

Fielding soccer, in which two teams throw a cricket ball and try to score goals – much like a game of soccer – is not my favourite exercise. It was the same exercise in which I hurt my knee and had to go home early from the Ashes tour in 1997.

Jones was just 25 when he hurt his knee and feared for some months that his promising career would be over. He had played 45 one-day internationals at that point, was averaging better than 40 after scoring three centuries at the start of that year, and was regarded as one of the best batsmen in the world. But now everything had come crashing down and in its place he was left with just bitter disappointment and the need to work harder than ever before simply to play again.

Jones was dedicated and his hard work enabled him to return and even surpass his previous achievements, but it meant he was reluctant to put the stress on the knee joint that would come from turning in orthodox fashion. Eventually, Jones became comfortable with turning blind and found that by bouncing into the turns against his stronger right knee, he could even gain a fraction of a second for the next run.

But remember, he would sum up the situation as he was running the first run, and would analyse it again as he came back for the second, so it was only rare occasions that he would find himself in trouble because he had turned blind. Even so, I recommend that you stick with the orthodox technique.

Hard running in turn puts pressure on the fieldsmen. Instead of them having the luxury of being able to get across to the ball, get behind it to stop it going to the boundary, take a few steps to get balanced, then wind up and throw it back in, they would have to sprint to it, try to pick it up at full pace and then get a flat, hard throw in while they are off-balance. This causes fieldsmen to cut corners to prevent the second run. Often they start to creep in a few metres to enable them to get to the ball quicker – meaning a firm shot wide or over their heads will no longer be reachable, but will probably go to the fence. And they may start to watch the batsman to see what he is doing rather than keeping their eye on the ball to guarantee they gather it. Errors start to occur when the fieldsman stops watching the ball. He might miss the ball completely or fail to pick it up. His throw might go wide or he might even pick the wrong end to throw to in a desperate bid to counter the hard-running batsmen. These all create little victories for the batsmen that arise simply because they run hard when the ball goes into the outfield.

The second way to gain a victory over the fielding team is to take the pace off the ball and run quick singles from shots that are essentially defensive strokes. Big hitting is immediately associated with one-day cricket, but short singles are easily as much a part of the game. Players like Ponting and Bevan are brilliant at taking runs and rotating the strike this way.

Using soft hands, they drop the ball almost at the feet and immediately dash through for runs that, more often than not, turn into easy singles as the fieldsmen realise they cannot prevent the run. Communication is vital. Both batsmen need to respond immediately to their partner's call – hesitation can be fatal. The fieldsmen are like sharks as they converge on the ball and only have to throw it a few metres to the stumps. But they are rarely closer than 15 metres from the bat, so even if the ball drops straight down and doesn't even roll off the pitch, the batsmen usually have enough time to get through.

This is not a new technique. Australian Test openers Bob Simpson and Bill Lawry were famous for their understanding and ability to rotate the strike with quick singles and hard running when they played together in the 1960s. It is no coincidence that Simmo was so keen to improve this aspect of the Australian one-day game during his ten years as coach of the team. He knew it was an area in which the team could pick up ten or 20 more runs an innings without taking great risks.

Practise these shots in the nets. Become familiar with getting into position, then softening your hands to make sure the ball has no pace on it. Bevan practises this skill every time he's in a net. He sets the field in his mind and then tries to bat so his defensive shots go between the fieldsmen. Jones used to do the same thing. It is practising the mental part of the game as much as the physical by being ready and looking to stamp your mark on the game. Practise as you play is the old saying, and if you practise well enough, you can't help but play better.

Aggression doesn't have to translate into big, thumping shots, but can be identified in a batsman who refuses to be tied down and looks for singles off every ball. In fact, it can be quite intimidating for a bowler running up to the wicket knowing that he could bowl an over consisting of nothing but good deliveries and still comfortably give up four or five runs. And if you reckon there is no aggression on the field when that happens a few times, have a look at the bowler tearing his hair out and staring at his fieldsmen while muttering vile curses to himself.

I emphasise in this book that being versatile and creative is essential in one-day cricket. The good players have realised that breaking up the field and frustrating the bowlers by taking these short singles is one of the best ways to achieve those aims. And it is a good way to counter a bowler who is in good rhythm and has you tied down. If they are on song, top-quality bowlers like Curtly Ambrose and Allan Donald are unlikely to bowl many, if any, bad balls that you can set yourself to hit to the boundary. They will nag away at a good line and length, at tremendous pace, of course, and demand that the batsman takes a big risk to play attacking shots. You still need to score though, as well as rotate the strike to prevent inertia overcoming the innings. Using defensive shots as a method of scoring becomes very valuable.

The non-striker plays a crucial role in these singles. Often, he will be running to the danger end because it is rare that a close fieldsman tearing in at full pace towards the striker's end will be able to gather the ball, change direction and hurl it to the bowler's stumps. Although the ball may be played in front of the wicket, and naturally appear to be the striker's call, the non-striker is likely to have to decide if the run is on.

The striker may be on the back-foot and may not have any momentum as he plays the stroke, so he is relying on his partner to assess the situation and call him through. That's where teamwork, communication and knowing how your partner will respond becomes so vital. We may not have showed it when we first batted together at the top of the order, but after 40-odd innings together, Mark Waugh and I are starting to work out each other's game pretty well.

Here's another trick worth trying. I don't know many teams that try it, but I think it is worthwhile to time your speed between wickets. Dean Jones knew it would take him just a fraction under ten seconds to run three and although it may have looked as though he had hyperactive electricity surging through his veins, he actually had a good idea if the runs were on as soon as the shot was played. He knew his own game – and that of his teammates – and could take advantage of that knowledge.

If, for example, Tom Moody knows it takes him 8 seconds to run two, and Michael Bevan can do it in 7 seconds, they are better able to work out which runs are risky and which ones can be more easily achieved. If Bevan hits the ball to fine leg, he knows he has 7 seconds to come back to the danger end to finish the second run. Moody is not running to the danger end so his slower pace is no hindrance to taking the second run. If, however, Moody hit the ball and Bevan was backing up, the pair would know that taking two is more likely to put Tom in danger and they can weigh up whether the risk is worthwhile.

Time yourself and your teammates for singles, twos, threes and even fours, though all-run fours are pretty rare in one-day cricket with the extra fieldsmen sweeping the boundaries. Then time how long it takes for a ball struck from the bat to reach the fieldsman and be returned to the stumps. You might be surprised at the number of runs you can pick up by simply running to your ability. Too often, batsmen dawdle between the stumps because they think there is only a single to be taken when, in fact, hard running could create a relatively easy two.

One-day cricket is a game of percentages, and running between wickets is one of those areas where the percentages can be improved most readily and add up to the batting team's benefit.

# Setting Targets

Some captains and coaches like to set targets for their batsmen to reach. They want 80 on the board after 20 overs, they say. Or, they want to score at four an over until the last five overs when happy hour starts. They apply the same thinking when they are batting second and chasing a total. Chasing 180, for example, requires that the team only has to bat at just under four an over to get there.

Or, if chasing a big total, they try to set interim figures along the way. If the target is 250, being 0–50 after 15 and then two or three for 125 after 30 overs should ensure a successful chase. That is all very well, but it is possible to fall into a trap by concentrating on the figures themselves and not on the game.

Australia tends to play it more by ear these days and assesses the situation every few overs. I guess that's the advantage of having an experienced team that has seen plenty of different match scenarios, but even so, there is no reason that any team should be uptight about having a set target and then not being able to stick to it. In general, you know how much a pitch and outfield are worth.

Sharjah, with its billiard-table outfield and a pitch that would not be out of place running across the Nullarbor between Perth and Adelaide, regularly gives up scores of 300. So, too, Adelaide Oval, with its short boundaries and true surface.

But Sydney and Manchester are different. Some days, looking at the conditions at those grounds, you know straight away that 220 might be enough to win the game.

Rather than simply eyeing a target, which I suppose is similar to a mountain climber concentrating on standing at the top of Mt Everest rather than thinking about the thousands of individual steps required to get there, Steve Waugh and Geoff Marsh are big on updating the score required as you go along. It's more like the climber saying: 'Let's get to the next slope on the mountain before dark, then we will assess our options.'

The same applies when you are batting. If the score is rattling along at eight an over in the first ten, you know you have got plenty in the bank already and you don't have to panic if the rate slows with the fall of a wicket or two. Or if you are chasing 220 and have raced to 75 off 12, you know you are going well and don't have to bust a boiler the whole way. On the other hand, if you are behind the rate that commonsense dictates you will need to maintain to overhaul a target, you might have to push it along in the middle of the innings to prevent the target getting away from you. If you need 200 off 40 overs after dawdling along at one an over, time will start to get away from you unless you can pick up the scoring. Instead of setting targets and trying to achieve them, you adjust as you go.

I tend to go about it that way in my own game. Some batsmen think the small targets set along the road as milestones to be ticked off are more important than the overall result. They can become more concerned with achieving specific goals every five overs or so than they are about just playing each ball as it deserves. But there is rarely any need to panic in one-day cricket, particularly if you have wickets in hand.

If you have scraped to 8 after five overs, you will know if it is because you have missed chances to score or if the opposition has bowled really well and denied you opportunities. If they have bowled well, you might have to see off the spell and wait for a new bowler to come on.

Or perhaps you are not taking the initiative to get the scoreboard moving and can improve matters by pushing a few quick singles or weighing up your options and deciding on a short onslaught on a particular bowler.

## Reverse Sweep

One of the ways that batsmen take the initiative is to play unorthodox shots, such as the reverse sweep. What the cleverly disguised slow ball is to the bowling side of one-day cricket, the reverse sweep is to batting. Until recently, the reverse sweep was seen as a novelty – a comic attempt by batsmen to disrupt the concentration of bowlers – as much as it was designed to score runs. Yet now it is recognised as much more valuable than that, and has gone well past the stage of being considered a joke.

The first time Australians really saw a reverse sweep was at the famous World Cup final in Calcutta in 1987. Mike Gatting was the player and he had England comfortably placed at 2–135 to overhaul Australia's total of 253 when Allan Border sent down his first ball of the match. Unless the bowler sends down a rank full toss or long hop first up, a well-placed batsman would normally take a ball or two to assess the situation before starting his assault. But Gatting, who was so keen to demonstrate his authority over his fellow captain, decided to bring his new toy out of the box immediately.

73

THE REVERSE SWEEP IS NOW A SHARP WEAPON IN A BATSMAN'S ARMOURY. IT IS EXECUTED BY TURNING YOUR HANDS OVER, KEEPING YOUR EYES OVER THE BALL AND HITTING DOWN ON IT LIKE A NORMAL SWEEP SHOT. PRACTICE WILL MAKE PERFECT.

74

The psychological benefit of reverse-sweeping the opposition captain for four from the first ball would have been incalculable. And with Gatting intending to hit towards backward point with the natural angle of Border's left-arm orthodox spinners, it appeared to be a reasonably safe bet. Gatting's planning might have had merit, but his execution was disastrous.

**Mike Gatting**
Born 6/6/57
92 matches 88 innings 17 not out 2095 runs
115* highest score 29.51 average 1x100 9x50

The ball was in the perfect position just outside off-stump but, unfortunately for Gatting, instead of sitting up and being belted past point to the boundary, it bounced a fraction more than he expected and ballooned off the top edge to wicketkeeper Greg Dyer. Tom Moody, who was in the Australian squad, recalls the moment: 'We couldn't believe you could play such a shot. As it turns out, it could have cost them the World Cup because Gatting was batting superbly and they lost momentum when he got out.'

The shot had been around for a few years when Gatting tried it on the biggest stage in world cricket, but its full potential had not yet been recognised. In 1981, Javed Miandad, the cheeky Pakistan champion who is regarded as one of the best one-day players ever, arrived at Glamorgan to play county cricket. Miandad was known for his sparkling footwork, his constant chatter and his innovative batsmanship, and he didn't waste any time taking the attack to county bowlers. One of his methods was to employ the reverse sweep to counter negative field settings and tight bowling. Given his exquisite skills that allowed him to use his bat like a magic wand,

Miandad soon demonstrated that the sweep was a sharp weapon that could really disrupt the bowlers.

It was then taken up by county batsmen who had the time and opportunity to tinker with traditional aspects of the game. The reverse sweep has reached fruition this decade under the influence of several high-profile players who decided to employ it for the same reason Miandad had – to counter field placings and tight bowling.

Many South Africans play the reverse sweep, partly a legacy of former England all-rounder Bob Woolmer who coached there in the 1990s. Woolmer, who has been an innovator much like Miandad a decade or more earlier, encouraged players like Hansie Cronje, Jonty Rhodes and Jacques Kallis to play reverse sweeps. They took to it like ducks to water. I had a bird's-eye view as Rhodes played several bullet-like sweeps that smashed into the point boundary in matches at the SCG in 1998. He hit the shot as hard as a normal sweep and rarely gave the fieldsmen a chance of cutting it off.

In England, all-rounder Dermot Reeve, playing in the 1992 and 1996 World Cups, used the reverse sweep as a regular attacking shot. It is commonplace in the one-day competitions in England, with all-rounder Adam Hollioake probably the best exponent at present. But he has a fair way to go to match Durham's Martin Speight who showed how the reverse sweep has become an orthodox batting stroke by playing it six times in an over in a one-day match against Kent in 1998. Dean Jones, who was an instigator and refiner of many elements of one-day cricket in Australia, has played the shot a bit, and Darren Lehmann, a flexible and attacking one-day batsman, is probably the best reverse sweeper going around now.

Jones, in fact, first tried it in the same World Cup series in which Gatting came to grief. The match was at Indore and Australia eventually beat New Zealand by three runs. Jones tried the shot once, but put it away for the rest of the tournament after receiving a curt message from coach Bob Simpson that if he wanted to reverse sweep, he could wave goodbye to playing for his country again. Perhaps that was lucky. Gatting played his notorious shot only two weeks later and not only gave Australia the World Cup, but carved his own place in cricket history.

Poor Gatt. Apart from playing the most infamous shot in the history of the game, he is also remembered for being on the receiving end of Shane Warne's ball of the century. Despite that, Gatting was a fine one-day player whose total of 2095 runs for England still puts him in his country's top eight one-day run scorers.

Lehmann, of course, has played a fair bit of cricket in England. Allied to the lack of bounce on his home pitch at Adelaide Oval, he has discovered the reverse sweep is well suited to his attacking game plan. He is an innovative and aggressive player, but he is only doing something that feels natural for him. He feels confident of playing it well because he has tried it in different circumstances.

He played it very well in Grenada in the West Indies in April 1999 as he belted and nudged his way to a superb 110 not out. Again, he picked the right conditions and the right ball.

**Darren Lehmann**
Born 5/2/70
59 matches 55 innings 8 not out 1527 runs
110* highest score 32.48 average 2x100 8x50

The pitch was quite flat and though it turned a little bit it didn't have a lot of bounce, so Lehmann was able to get on top of the ball and not have to worry that a delivery might jump more than he expected. He missed with his first attempt or two, then managed to steer a couple away for ones and twos before finally getting his eye in. He then used the reverse sweep to bludgeon the spin bowlers, particularly the West Indies part-timer Keith Arthurton, and exploit the large vacant areas behind point.

The reverse sweep is better suited to turning pitches rather than those that bounce, so it is more regularly played in England and the subcontinent. The harder pitches in Australia provide less opportunities to play it because the natural enemy of the shot is not the ball that turns, but the one that bounces. Nevertheless, as Rhodes showed, it is a deadly weapon if the conditions are suitable or the player can hit it well enough.

Like every shot, it must be practised. Rhodes, Lehmann and the English exponents practise it over and over in the nets so that just like a forward defensive shot, or a cover drive, it becomes second nature. And they try it against different types of bowlers – they learn who it is better suited to playing against. The shot is dangerous because it has to be premeditated – some batsmen like to swap hands on the bat, so they need time to get into position.

Others simply turn their hands over and swat towards gully. Either method puts the batsman at the mercy of the delivery, particularly if it is a bit quicker and straighter than expected. But there is no question about its effectiveness. It exploits a situation that we cover in the Fielding chapter. If bowlers are working to their plan and giving the batsman little to hit outside off-stump, the area square and behind on the off-side can be patrolled by just one fieldsman. That is fertile space for a batsman looking for an area to score. As the game has evolved sophisticated fielding strategies, so too have the steps to counter it. This is where the reverse sweep is so valuable. It's a way of manipulating the field – if you want to force the field squarer to open up opportunities straighter down the ground, it's a good way to do it.

Playing the reverse sweep is not technically very different from the orthodox sweep shot. The front foot should go across towards the pitch of the delivery. You must keep your eye on the ball, then hit down on it to direct it behind point. It is a temptation for a batsman to lift his head when he plays the stroke – he is naturally concerned that the ball might bounce or come off a top edge and hit him in the face.

Yet by keeping the head down and virtually sniffing the ball, the chances of being hit are dramatically reduced. Instead, the batsman will find he is more likely to hit it in the middle of the bat because he will have his eyes closer to the point of impact than with most other shots.

The sweep is different to the lap – a shot that can be played in both orthodox and reverse fashion by angling the bat and simply guiding the ball so that it runs away through its own pace. The orthodox lap is little different to the reverse lap, except that the ball is struck towards fine leg rather than third man. Using the pace of the delivery, you point the toe of the bat towards the line of the ball and simply allow it to run along the face of the bat and past the wicketkeeper.

While you should roll your wrists as you play a sweep so that the ball stays on the ground, you don't need to for a lap shot. In fact, batsman are usually happy for the ball to go in the air because they are hitting into an area without any catching fieldsmen. It can be used to hit the ball fine on the leg-side from the line of the stumps, or even outside off-stump or, with the reverse lap, hit through the slips from the same ball.

If you are going to play reverse sweeps or laps, I recommend you practise in the nets until you feel comfortable with the shot. And don't just play it off the last ball or two of a net session. If you are serious about playing the shot, get a teammate to throw plenty of balls to you so that you can work on your footwork, how you position your hands and on keeping your head down. Remember, practise well and you will play better.

# Crease Management

'Crease management' – it's an odd term and sounds like something invented by a well-paid business consultant who wears bow-ties and braces. It is a useful phrase covering the many elements a batsman has to deal with at the crease. It's also a useful way of storing them together in the memory. Dean Jones invented the term to describe the various elements of batting.

Crease management takes in such things as the monitoring of your equipment, so that you are alert to the need to change your gloves if they get sweaty, or tighten your helmet strap if it comes loose and causes the helmet to shift around on your head. It also covers how you analyse the game. Is the bowler changing his pace or occasionally going wider on the crease when he delivers? Are there five fieldsmen on the fence or has one come up to short fine leg? Are you relaxing between balls or are you tensing up and finding it hard to concentrate?

Basically, crease management is everything that happens to you as a batsman other than the actual batting – the footwork, shot selection, ball striking, placement and running – part of your innings. If you are a good crease manager, it means you are in control of things and only have to worry about getting bat on ball. That's the essence of good batting. If the only thing in your mind is the task of getting bat on ball, and that's fundamentally what cricket is all about, you will succeed more often than if your head is cluttered with extraneous things.

# 2

# Bowling

The aim of bowlers is to take wickets. Or is it?

One-day cricket has created such a shift in the way the game is played that the natural aim of every bowler – to take wickets as regularly and as often as possible – has changed quite dramatically. In one-day cricket, run saving becomes an equally vital objective. That's not to say that bowlers shouldn't try to get wickets. There is no better way to reduce the run rate and put pressure on a batting team than to knock over a batsman or two. But the desire to take wickets in one-day cricket has to be balanced with the need to stay on top of the run rate. An opening bowler who can be relied on to produce less than 30 runs off ten overs is as vital a member of the team structure as a fiery quick like Glenn McGrath who will blast out three batsmen, but who may occasionally do so at the cost of 50 runs.

Australian opener Adam Dale is the perfect example of the straight man who is rarely in the limelight, but still plays a crucial role for his team. He has never terrified a batsman in his life, but he is so reliable at bowling straight at off-stump on a good length that he is always one of the first players

81

picked. Captain Steve Waugh knows that when he throws Dale the new ball, the batsmen are only going to score about 30 runs. Trying to get more will only put their wickets at risk.

Dale has the most important asset available to a one-day bowler — the ability to bowl line and length. And he hits the seam often enough to do a little bit both ways and keep the batsmen in two minds. He is a patient bowler, too. He is prepared to keep hitting the spot because he knows his job is just to bowl 60 tight deliveries.

**Adam Dale**
Born 30/12/68
27 matches 237 overs 29 maidens 901 runs 29 wickets
31.06 average 3–18 best bowling 49.0 strike rate
3.80 runs per over

In a Test match, nine out of ten batsmen are happy to ride a tough period through. They have four or five days to play, so they just acknowledge that the bowler is doing well, knuckle down to keep the good balls out and simply wait for the bowler to lose patience. But in one-day cricket, there is no reason for the bowler to lose patience. He only has ten overs to bowl and he would be happy to bowl those 60 deliveries with the batsman blocking each one of them. That's where the batsman has to be innovative to throw the bowler off the line. As soon as he tries to do that, though, he gives the bowler the chance to knock him over.

That's what Adam Dale does and it explains why he is one of the most effective one-day bowlers around. If batsmen want to take him on, they do so at their own risk. In fact, Dale only got collared once during his superb 1998/99 season when he was the epitome of accuracy. This took place at the WACA when flamboyant Sri Lankan opener Sanath Jayasuriya hit through the line consistently and took 34 off Dale's first four overs. That really was an exception though, and Jayasuriya is one of only a handful of batsmen in the world who could have taken on such an accurate bowler and won the battle.

Dale did not have as good a 1999 World Cup campaign, playing only the two matches and only taking one wicket. But he still only gave up 50 runs in the 15 overs that he bowled, meaning his niggardly accuracy was still difficult to get away. His absence from the team was more a reflection on Australia's changing strategy and the fact that conditions in England were better suited to opening bowlers whose job it was to strike hard for wickets.

Although all of that was tough for Dale, don't be surprised to see him bounce back and continue to frustrate batsmen the world over.

# Attacking by Defence

One of the best ways to build pressure on batsmen is to attack by defence – to maintain protection in the field rather than employ an overt attacking strategy. The hardest thing for a batsman in one-day cricket is to come to the crease and get going immediately. Determining the pace of the pitch and what the bowlers are doing can take a few overs, so the fielding team needs to interrupt that momentum by having the right field in place and the right bowlers in action. This increases the chances of taking a wicket. Restricting a batsman to just two or three off 20 balls is a lot more likely to get him out than employing three slips and a gully and trying to create an edge.

The captain has to make sure the bowler is aware of the batsman's strengths and weaknesses so he knows exactly what line and length to bowl to the field that has been set. The bowlers will be instructed that if a certain batsman comes to the crease, they should try to bowl as many dot-balls to him as possible in the next 30 minutes. The batsman might then play a stupid shot and get out – it is not the leg-cutter that will get him out, but the pressure on him. That pressure might lead to him playing a drive that he wouldn't normally play.

Against England, the Australians tend to place a short midwicket to Alec Stewart – because he likes to play through there – and then concentrate on bowling very straight. The combination tends to frustrate Stewart because it restricts him from playing one of his most profitable shots and, on the odd occasion, he has hit a catch to that position.

If the conditions are really suited to bowling, that is, the ball is swinging or seaming around, a team can be a little more aggressive by using two slips for a while. But that would not last long.

Most teams have their version of Adam Dale, though few do it as well as he does. In England, Angus Fraser is a classic example of a containing tight seamer who can be relied on to bowl ten solid overs. And slow medium-pacer Chris Harris, of New Zealand, has made an artform of constricting the run rate and giving nothing away.

# Accuracy

Whether you are a fast bowler, a leg-spinner or medium-pacer, one-day cricket demands accuracy – the ability to bowl in the same spot all day. If you can't bowl on a good length at the stumps, or just outside off-stump, batsmen will hit you all over the ground. Even the best strike bowlers in the world are not safe if they stray in their accuracy. Glenn

McGrath, Allan Donald and Waqar Younis might be able to spear through the best batsmen in the world, but if they don't bowl straight, their extra speed means they get hit as often and perhaps more than moderate medium-pacers.

| | Matches | Wickets | Strike rate | Economy per over |
|---|---|---|---|---|
| **Waqar Younis** | 172 | 285 | 30.2 | 4.5 |
| **Allan Donald** | 121 | 206 | 31.2 | 4.0 |
| **Glenn McGrath** | 99 | 144 | 37.1 | 4.0 |

Accuracy is crucial. It means the captain can set the most appropriate field for the situation, confident in the knowledge that his bowler will put it in the right spot. If the bowler does not have great control, the captain is limited in his ability to set the best fields. Even very attacking bowlers like McGrath, whose primary job is to take wickets, has to temper his aggression and seek to bowl on the spot for most of his spell. His first aim is still to blast out two or three batsman at the top of the order. Even then, he relies on his accuracy and ability to build pressure on the batsmen as one of his greatest weapons.

A fielding captain is never happier than when he has two bowlers drying up the runs at each end by sticking to a good line and length. When you stop the runs at both ends, things start to happen for the fielding team. Batsmen start doing silly things – they play risky shots to good balls and look for runs that aren't quite there. Run-outs happen, batsmen take risky singles and attempt shots that aren't on after both bowlers have kept things tight for four or five overs. This demonstrates how the captain, the bowlers and the fieldsmen have to work as a team to take wickets and restrict the run flow.

# Teamwork and Partnerships

West Australian captain, Tom Moody, who is one of the most experienced limited-overs players in the world, has a great saying that sums up how bowlers should approach the one-day environment. He says: 'I want bowlers to bowl in partnerships and fieldsmen to hunt in packs.' By bowling in partnerships, Tom means he wants the bowlers to work together to build pressure on the batsman. If one bowler is more attacking, therefore more likely to create a catch or wicket opportunity, but also more likely to get hit for runs, his partner should think to himself, 'Right, I'll make sure I keep it tight at my end so that between us, we don't go for too many runs.'

The same applies if you know a batsman wants to play a certain range of shots. Say, for example, he is a keen cutter, or scores many of his runs by driving though the covers. The bowlers can build the pressure on him by concentrating on bowling at middle-stump to deny those favourite strokes and, eventually, will more than likely force him to take risks to score some runs. Both bowlers need to work as a team to achieve this.

I know, to my cost, how effective this tactic can be. Last summer, both Alan Mullally and Darren Gough worked very hard on bowling straight to me to prevent me playing the cut that has been such a good source of runs for me over my career. They both did it so well in several matches that I ended up trying a risky shot and chopped the ball onto my stumps.

If batsmen realise that one bowler is sending down plenty of loose stuff, they don't have to take risks against his tighter partner and the pressure is released. When you build pressure like that, wicket opportunities develop automatically.

It is attack by defence. But if one end is going well and the other end is giving up six runs an over, the fielding team will struggle to achieve anything.

Ideally, both ends will create that pressure. McGrath and Dale work superbly in partnership to build pressure. Dale plugs away on a good line and length, and while McGrath does pretty much the same, his extra pace means that occasionally he could try to put a quicker ball though the batsman and surprise him into playing a poor shot. Between the two of them, it is rare for a batting team to get off to a good start.

The second half of Tom Moody's message applies to the fieldsmen. We will look at their role in more detail in Fielding (pages 149–76) but it is fair to say that the success of any bowler depends on the good work of the other ten men in the field. Fieldsmen need to be in tune with what is happening in the game because they can assist the bowlers to create the pressure that leads to wickets. If, say, McGrath is bowling well to England opener Alec Stewart, and the dashing right-hander is becoming tied down, he will think to himself, 'I'm going to have to take the pace off the ball here. I'll try to drop one at my feet and get one so that I am off strike.'

Ricky Ponting, at point, should be able to read that situation and be aware that he is likely to have to dash in on a short single. Conversely, if he stays ahead of the play and prevents Stewart getting off strike, the batsman might play a poor shot later in the over and knock up a catch.

Depriving the batting side of runs and the consequent building of pressure creates wickets. It is amazing the number of times you see a good bowling partnership create a run-out. The batsmen don't know where the next run is coming from, they are not receiving any bad balls to put away, the captain has set the field in the exact positions to stop any shots that are played and the fieldsmen are alert and ready to

87

pounce on any ball that comes their way. No wonder the batsmen become desperate and throw their wickets away by attempting a suicidal run.

Bowlers should not be afraid to give away a run or two at the end of an over if it means they can prevent a boundary. If they have bowled four dot-balls, or have given up no more than one or two runs, it makes sense to minimise run-scoring chances for the rest of the over. The fieldsmen in the ring can go back to the line and concede a single if the ball is played to them. The over might cost three or four, but the chance of a boundary being hit is reduced. Make it a tidy over that builds pressure on the batsmen.

The same principle applies to the variety a bowler will employ. It might be better to try the variety earlier in the over but concentrate on bowling at the spot towards the end. A bowler's normal thought pattern might be that if he has bowled a tight over, the pressure is on the batsman and it might be worth attacking him. But that tactic can backfire. If you attack and they get four, you feel as though all the work has been for nothing and the pressure subsides. Don't be afraid to tighten the screws on the batsman, get a maiden over and force them to attack next time. Maintaining pressure is the key. It is a commonsense tactic to push the field back to protect the last ball or two of a good over.

Good bowlers with great control will often bowl four or five balls for few runs, then work extra hard to put the ball on the spot. They are trying both to prevent a run being scored and to force the batsman to play a risky shot.

# Change Bowlers

A good bowling partnership does not necessarily mean using the team's best bowlers in tandem, but rather pairing them in such a way as to maintain maximum pressure for as long as possible. This means that sometimes the best fast bowler will not take the new ball or a spinner might open the innings. Have a look at South Africa's strategy in using Allan Donald as a first or second change bowler. There are special reasons South Africa has tried this approach and it has been remarkably successful for them.

Of course, they have such a good fast attack with players like Shaun Pollock, Jacques Kallis and Lance Klusener that they can afford the luxury of keeping their premier bowler from the crease until the 15th or 20th over.

Many teams can't afford to do this but even so, there is nothing stopping the principle being used at all levels. There is no reason the fastest bowler should automatically take the new ball. One-day cricket changes so much during a match that sticking to a formula developed a decade or more ago may no longer be so strictly applied.

Let's have a closer look at Donald, the man known as 'White Lightning', and the reasons he has been so successful as a change bowler. There is no doubt he is quick. He bowls at 150 kilometres per hour – about top pace for quicks around the world – and doesn't allow any batsmen to be totally comfortable at the crease. So Donald can be used to maintain pressure through the middle of the innings. This is the time the batting side is trying to consolidate if it has made a good start, or it is starting to build momentum towards a winning score if it started slowly. Donald puts enormous pressure on the batsmen during overs 15 to 35. That is the time the team wants to accumulate four or five runs an over, but with Donald flying in at one end and taking wickets, it is hard for the batsmen to achieve it. He is difficult to get away because of his pace and bounce, but he is also likely to take wickets. In fact, it is his attacking nature that perhaps led South Africa to replace him as a new ball bowler.

**Allan Donald**
Born 20/10/66
121 matches 1073 overs 76 maidens 4336 runs 206 wickets
21.04 average 6–23 best bowling 31.2 strike rate
4.04 runs per over

Donald didn't have as good a record in one-dayers until he started coming on as first or second change. Perhaps because of his attacking nature, he was the type of bowler who was always looking for a wicket, and so became expensive and less effective. With the field up and the new ball swinging around, he found he didn't get the rewards if he got the batsmen to edge the ball. He also gave up runs at a fast rate. And he tended not to vary things much – he would charge in and try to blast out batsmen as he has done so effectively at Test level. But he is very effective at one-day level now. He is quicker than Pollock, for example, so the intensity, instead of dropping back when the opening bowler goes off, lifts when he is replaced. Normally, if you have negotiated ten or 15 overs against the new ball, you can set yourself for a big score. But in South Africa's case, the pressure just becomes more intense.

South Africa's tactic is to often throw Klusener the new ball. He is quick and swings the ball, but doesn't have the control that Donald has. If Klusener breaks through and picks up two or three wickets, he has done a great job. If he doesn't go so well, they still have Donald up their sleeve. As one of the keys to success in one-day cricket is to try to keep your momentum a couple of overs ahead of the opposition, it is a remarkably successful tactic because it can take that one or two overs to adjust to Donald's extra pace. Klusener demonstrated his value early in South Africa's series in December 1997 when he virtually won a match against Australia in Melbourne.

Coincidentally, that was Tom Moody's first match back in the Australian team in almost a year and he bowled well to take 1–10 off his eight overs. But it was Klusener who stole the show. After scoring a brisk 17 batting at No. 3, he took the new ball and imposed himself immediately. He got Michael Di Venuto in his first over, snared Steve Waugh a few balls later and picked up Ricky Ponting as well. Australia slumped to 3–38. Klusener picked up the last two to finish with 5–24 and deservedly picked up the Man of the Match award. Klusener then showed his great allround value in the 1999 World Cup by putting bowling attacks to the sword while picking up 17 wickets of his own.

Donald has changed his role in one-day cricket over the years so that he not quite so attacking. He attacks by defence. He builds pressure on the batsman and forces the risk. And Donald knows that with quicksilver players like Jonty Rhodes and Herschelle Gibbs waiting in the covers, he can bowl a good line and length and the batsmen are going to struggle to pierce the field. Even bad balls may not get through because of the quality of the fieldsmen. This strategy forces the batsmen to take enormous risks and is one of the reasons South Africa has been so successful since they were readmitted to world cricket at the start of the 1990s.

# Choice of Bowlers

Which bowlers are called on depends on the opposition and the conditions. A humid, overcast day in Brisbane, for example, will call for a couple of swing bowlers to be used early in the innings in a bid to take wickets while the ball is hooping around. But one-day cricket is tough for genuine swing bowlers like Damien Fleming. He is reluctant to go for big swingers because he knows he is vulnerable, both to wide calls and batsmen trying to play attacking shots. And the absence of more than

91

two slips means that even if he beats the bat with a late outswinger, there is less chance of getting a catch caught. He might, say, bowl a big inswinger a couple of times. He knows the batsman is looking to swing it away to the leg-side and he could be hit for a couple of fours. Or he will get called for wides. It's tough work being a swing expert in one-dayers. A swing bowler will rarely have more than two slips, so there is less reward for beating the bat. But if he runs through a team, he can be a match-winner. Fleming, in particular, has done well in India and Pakistan – although the ball swings, it rarely goes as far as in Australia or England where the conditions are more swing-friendly. This means Fleming can get the ball to do enough to beat the bat, but it won't go so far that it can be picked off. Fleming had a superb World Cup in India and Pakistan in 1996 because of that, including taking a match-winning 5–36 against India in the qualifying match in Bombay when a rampaging Sachin Tendulkar threatened to win the match single-handedly for his country. It is one of the quirks of the game that Fleming has played 61 one-dayers but only nine in Australia. But he has been invaluable in the subcontinent and Sharjah, where he regularly performs well.

**Damien Fleming**
Born 24/4/70
64 matches 558.5 overs 42 maidens 2437 runs 99 wickets
24.61 average 5–36 best bowling 33.8 strike rate
4.36 runs per over

Another tactic that has worked well is to open with a spinner. In 1992, New Zealand used off-spinner Dipak Patel to open in its World Cup matches. The astute Kiwi captain Martin Crowe was covering for a lack of depth in New Zealand's bowling by holding back a medium-pacer for later in the innings, when the batsmen were looking to push the runs along. It also was a good surprise move because it forced the batsmen to change their thinking.

The slow pitches of New Zealand were well suited to the tactic because the ball did not come on and the batsmen were forced to make the pace. They had to play risky shots over the infield. The key to the move was Patel's accuracy. He bowled a nagging line and length which made it difficult for the batsmen to play attacking shots. If he had been loose, the theory could have backfired badly. It was suited to the conditions, too. This strategy may not work as well on other grounds where the bounce and pace of the pitch allow batsmen to hit through the off-spinner's line.

However, bowlers can sometimes exploit these conditions. Pat Symcox took the new ball for South Africa in Perth in January 1998 and used the bounce of the pitch to great effect. Symcox, one of the most extroverted characters in the game, is a tall man who relies on his height almost as much as his ability to turn the ball. The bouncy pitch helped him take 1–16 in his six-over new ball spell – great figures considering he could only have two men outside the circle – and he finished with 2–33 off ten overs. Great work indeed, even if the second wicket was me, caught by Donald as I tried to smash a short ball over the infield, only to be surprised by the bounce and spoon it to mid-on.

Anil Kumble, the great Indian leg-spinner, opens on his home pitches occasionally. That is understandable, though, if the team includes three or four spinners. Bowling at a brisk medium pace, Kumble gets more bounce than turn. He is probably most dangerous with a hard new ball at the start of an innings in the subcontinent, rather than after 20 or 30 overs when it has become softer and won't get up as much. It is simply a matter of reading the conditions and using your bowling strengths accordingly.

Steve Waugh showed two could play at that game by using his brother Mark, a very respectable off-spinner with 81 one-day wickets at international level, to open in Sydney in the second final of the series against South Africa in 1998. Again, it worked superbly. Mark struck in his first over, enticing Daryll Cullinan to hit a full toss straight to mid-on. And who better to catch it than Shane Warne, whose grin went from ear to ear.

This was a fine example of unorthodox thinking paying off. It also showed the value of having a surprise card up your sleeve. But then Mark Waugh is a far better bowler than he sometimes gets credit for. Bob Simpson considers him to have enough raw talent to become an accomplished international off-spinner in his own right.

If it means the batting team takes two overs to adjust to these tactics, it has been a success.

# Versatility

Mark Waugh's success indicates another element of the game that all players should be aware of – the need to be versatile. It is no coincidence that some of the best one-day teams in the world – Australia, South Africa and Pakistan – have the most versatile line-ups.

Each team is jam-packed with all-rounders – players who can bat well and then be called on to bowl a few overs. This flexibility is a great advantage to a captain, particularly if he knows he can call on any one of eight or nine players to roll his arm over. In Australia's case, apart from the frontline bowlers like McGrath, Warne and Fleming, Steve Waugh can call on Ricky Ponting, Mark Waugh, Damien Martyn, Darren Lehmann, Michael Bevan or himself from the top of the batting line-up.

94

These players may not be called on for four or five games, but then, as Ponting found against Sri Lanka in Perth in January 1999, he might be required to bowl ten overs.

Ponting is a great example of a player adding another string or two to his bow. He is a tremendous one-day player already – he is a solid No. 3 batsman and, along with South Africa's Jonty Rhodes, one of the two best fieldsmen in the game – but he knows his bowling makes him even more valuable. At one level, he could win a game for his team with his wicket-taking ability as a bowler. He did that in Perth against the Sri Lankans after Jayasuriya had hit Dale out of the attack. Ponting was thrown the ball and responded by taking the prize wicket of Arjuna Ranatunga as he bowled a tight ten-over spell.

'To bowl ten overs was a bit of a surprise,' Ponting reflected after winning the Man of the Match award for his allround performance that saw him score 39, run out Marvan Atapattu with a searing direct hit, take a couple of athletic catches and trap Ranatunga with a seaming ball that he could only nick behind. 'But I thought I might bowl three or four and if I could be pretty cheap, that would be a bonus for the team. I always try to do the best I can with the ball.'

At the other end of the scale, and this is something all players should appreciate, Ponting knows he could retain or win his spot in the side simply because his bowling attributes put him ahead of another player who bats and fields equally well.

Even the slightest advantage could be vital for a player on the fringe of a team. If he works on his bowling, it may just give him the edge when the selectors are weighing up their options. The same applies to Martyn and Lehmann and other players. Ponting certainly works hard on his bowling so that, like in Perth, he is ready if and when he gets called up.

Ponting is always working on different things. He is a good cricketer and thinks about different aspects of the game. He bowls medium-pacers, which have brought him a couple of Test wickets, but he also bowls very good off-spinners.

You never know when you might get the chance to bowl in a game. There might be seven recognised bowlers in a team, but if one suffers an injury, and one or two others get hit around, the captain will be looking for other options. Darren Lehmann, for example, is another versatile player in the Ponting mould. He is picked as a batsman but with his skills, he can be called on when the team needs a change. He is not a recognised spinner but he is good enough to bowl a few overs. This worked superbly a couple of times on spinning pitches in Australia in the summer of 1997/98. In the final against South Africa at the MCG, where the pitch was doing a bit, he came on and almost turned the game enough for us to win when he took two wickets in as many overs.

And they were key batsmen he dismissed, too. He had Hansie Cronje hole out to Bevan for 29 and then forced an edge from Jonty Rhodes when he was on 21. Two top-line batsmen gone and a part-time bowler had earned his pay already. Lehmann was the seventh bowler used that day and his four-over spell of 2–17 was ideal.

Lehmann might have had no idea he was going to bowl that day, but, because he has done the work for the captain to have confidence in him, he was able to do the job. In the nets, he bowls properly and knows exactly what he can and can't do. His strength is his ability to bowl full and straight, which is the key to success in one-day cricket. He provides good variety with his left-arm spinners and though he might not bowl a lot, he is respected by batsmen because he is good enough to chip out good wickets.

Batsmen should never consider they are not good enough to bowl. Leave that to the keepers to think about while you practise hard on that part of your game.

96

You never know when you will be needed to save or win a game and, as many all-rounders have found, having another string to your bow reduces the pressure on you to perform at your specialist task.

# Death Bowlers

As a one-day match ebbs and flows, so too are different bowlers suited to different situations. One of the most specialised roles is that of the 'death bowler', the player who gets the vital task of bowling in the last five or so overs when the batsmen are looking to score off every ball.

It is a huge responsibility for a bowler to end the innings. Batsmen are not concerned about losing their wickets – their main job is to swing the bat and thrash for the eight or ten runs each over needed to boost the score or win the run chase. Batsman call it the 'happy hour', but bowlers, being more pragmatic and knowing the game is arranged against them, have come up with a darker description!

Generally, death bowlers are well known and have an enviable reputation for being specialists at stopping the run flow. But what a responsibility. Like many parts of the one-day game, it is difficult to plan the bowling strategy at the end.

The first-choice bowlers might have to be replaced if they have bowled well earlier and been used for more overs than originally thought.

The captain might have been planning to use a certain bowler at the end, but that player might have bowled some of his spell at the start or in the middle and was doing so well that the captain kept him on. Instead of bowling six overs, he might have bowled eight and can only bowl two at the end. So, players who ideally wouldn't bowl in overs

40 to 50 will have to bowl two or three overs. Ideally, everyone who bowls in the team should be prepared – whether it is the first over or the last.

All bowlers should be prepared for a call to the crease at the end of the innings. The key to success at the end is the ability to get the ball in the block hole regularly and to have a good slower ball. If the ball is full and straight, it is difficult to hit it anywhere but straight down the ground. Fields can be set for those shots.

The last thing a fielding side needs at this stage, though, is a bowler being too short or wide. Width, whether it is outside off-stump or leg-stump, gives the batsman room to swing over the infield. And bowling a short length means the batsman has the opportunity to get under it and hit it to or over the boundary. Being able to bowl slower balls is crucial, too, because it disrupts the momentum of the batsmen and prevents them from taking full toll of the bowling. We take a detailed look at slower balls on pages 117–26.

Steve Waugh was a superb death bowler during the 1980s – he showed that you don't have to be quick to be efficient. He was a brisk medium-pacer at top pace, but his greatest attribute was his control – both over himself and his direction. He became known as the Iceman because he kept cool, no matter how heated the situation in the middle became.

His heart might have been racing, but Waugh was always able to concentrate on the most important thing: putting the next delivery on the right spot. No matter what numbers were on the scoreboard and what had happened to the previous ball, Waugh put those distractions aside. He provided a great lesson in concentration and precision under pressure.

This is important. If you can stay calm and stick to your task, you will be able to bowl in the right spot. No matter how parlous the game seems, one good ball can turn the tide if it takes a vital wicket or prevents a boundary. Imagine the pressure on the batting team in the last few overs – they have to make the runs, after all – and the bowlers should be able to cope with the pressure on them.

Pace bowlers and medium-pacers tend to be used most as death bowlers. There is nothing stopping a spinner doing the same thing if his control is good enough, though few spinners in international cricket, apart from Shane Warne, tend to bowl at the end. Warne is the exception simply because he is such a good player. His control is phenomenal and his variety means the batsmen can never attack him with complete certainty.

The thinking with spinners at the end is that their lack of pace gives the batsmen the opportunity to get under the ball and swing it away. But that's not a cast-iron rule for every match. As all batsmen know, a drifting and turning ball is still pretty hard to hit. That's why players like West Indian Keith Arthurton and Englishman Ashley Giles, both left-arm finger spinners, bowled the last over in tight run chases against Australia during 1998/99. Arthurton was almost successful in an amazing match in Guyana that ended controversially in a tie when the crowd invaded the ground during the last ball. No one will forget the chaotic scenes as the stumps were stolen and Steve Waugh was buffeted as he tried to make his ground for the third run. That event was extraordinary and overshadows Arthurton's effort in bowling four dot-balls in that over to keep the West Indies in the game.

Extreme pace is not vitally important. Waugh was a very good death bowler because he bowled straight, not because he bowled fast. He got the ball in the block hole and he had a very good slower ball. Those are the main assets of a death bowler – being able to bowl full and straight with the surprise slower ball. The most important thing is for the bowler to put the ball in the area that it will be hit to the field. If he is bowling short, it can be hit anywhere but if he is bowling full and straight, the batsman can only hit it straight.

Bruce Reid was another good bowler at the end, though he was also pretty good in the beginning and the middle, so he seldom had any overs left by the end of the innings. He was good at the start because he had the ability to knock over good batsmen, regardless of the conditions. He could come back in the middle and be relied on to hit a line and length from the first ball. Generally, when things were getting away in the middle overs, he could come back and stem the run flow.

**Bruce Reid**
Born 14/3/63
61 matches 541.4 overs 63 maidens 2203 runs 63 wickets
34.97 average 5–53 best bowling 51.59 strike rate
4.07 runs per over

Glenn McGrath, who can get reverse swing from the old ball, is very difficult to get away in the last few overs. But few can match the Pakistan Express – Waqar Younis – whose game seems to be designed for bowling at the end of a one-day innings. Waqar gets uncanny reverse swing, jams it in at the toes of the batsman and bowls at 150 kilometres per hour. Whether you are batting at No. 1 or No. 9, he presents a tough challenge.

Generally, the only way a bowler like Waqar will get punished in the last few overs is by little inside edges that race past the keeper to the boundary. Waqar and other good death bowlers rarely get hit square or down the ground, so the captain knows where his runs will be scored and can set the field accordingly. The hardest thing for a captain at the death is to get the bowler to bowl to the area for which he has set the field.

If he bowls short of a length, the ball can end up anywhere. It is imperative to bowl full and straight, though for players like Waqar and McGrath who have genuine pace, the occasional shorter ball will keep the batsmen guessing without damaging the defensive effort too much. This depends on factors such as the pitch and the batsmen.

# Fast Bowlers

The genuine fast bowler has several roles to play in one-day cricket. When he takes the new ball, his first job is to attack. There is no better way to slow the run rate and prevent batting teams racking up big scores than by taking wickets. But in one-day cricket he doesn't have the luxury of being able to attack like he would in a Test match or four-day match.

In Test cricket and first-class games, Glenn McGrath will open the bowling and seek to take several wickets in his first spell. The captain will employ for him at least three slips, a gully and a short leg as catching fieldsmen. He may only have two fieldsmen saving singles. McGrath is on the attack all the time because it is his job to take wickets with the new ball. If he can expose the middle order early, he has done a great job. It is certainly fantastic if he can take two or three early wickets in a one-day innings, but the nature of the game means he is less likely to do that.

In one-day cricket, the pitch will probably have less life and will be more likely to favour the batsmen than it would in a four- or five-day match. Because the pitch needs only to last 100 overs, it will be harder, flatter, less grassy and provide less assistance to the bowlers than it would if it had to last five days. It will not provide as much bounce, nor sideways movement. This naturally favours the batsmen and allows them to play more of the attacking shots that have become the hallmark of one-day cricket.

Then there are the field settings. Instead of three or four slips, there may be only two – so if the batsman gets an edge, the ball is less likely to be caught. There is no short leg, so any balls thudded in short of a length and leaping towards the batsman's armpit are not going to be caught if he pops it up off the glove or splice of the bat. These attacking field positions are vacant because the fieldsmen are in the ring saving the singles or down on the third man fence stopping boundaries. They have to be there to save runs. Unlike a Test match, one-day batsmen will attack from the first ball. They walk to the crease thinking that unless the ball is so good that it must be defended, they will attack everything.

In first-class cricket, batsmen are more patient – they're prepared to sit and wait for the really bad ball to come along. If they get five good overs in a row in a first-class game, they will push them back to the bowler and simply wait for the right ball. That principle is acknowledged in the coaching manuals as treating every ball on its merits. One-day cricket does not allow that luxury. Even if 30 good balls are bowled, the batsmen must try to score off at least a third of them. They will play plenty of attacking shots and the fieldsmen need to be in defensive positions to prevent those shots racing away to the boundary.

Even if a batting team is wavering at 2–20, for example, you will rarely see a lot of catching positions employed. Being too attacking can sometimes backfire on the fielding team and few captains are keen to go on the attack for too long. If a new batsman comes in at 2–20 and is confronted by three slips, a gully and one under his nose at short leg, there is almost as much pressure on the bowler as the new batsman. If there is minimal protection in the field, there are plenty of gaps for the batsman to pick. If he hits a four, then another, he virtually grows another leg. The bowler felt he was on top, then suddenly the pressure shifts onto him to regain his line and length.

Another ploy not available to the attacking one-day fast bowler is to vary his attack by bowling the occasional wider ball or a series of bouncers. We take a look at bouncers and their role in the one-day arena in the section that follows.

In some circumstances, a fast bowler who has tied down a batsman in first-class cricket will send down a much wider ball in a bid to tempt a false shot and a nick behind the wicket. West Australian bowlers such as Brendon Julian and Jo Angel often use that tactic at the WACA. They know that the extra bounce at the WACA makes it difficult for the batsman to keep the ball down if he plays an attacking shot when they push the ball wider.

Their plan is to bowl straight for a period to build pressure on the batsman and then tempt him by bowling a wider delivery. He's likely to play a rash shot that ends with a nick through to me behind the stumps or to the slips or gully.

But that doesn't work as well in one-day cricket for two reasons. First, wide balls are more strictly penalised, of course, so the bowler is liable to be docked a run and have to bowl another ball if he is a fraction outside the strike zone outside off-stump. Secondly, the batsman is always on the lookout for anything capable of being hit through or over the infield. In this case, the wider delivery is not a tempting surprise ball but a gift that few good batsmen will fail to use to full advantage.

## Bouncers

One-day cricket has evolved remarkably over the past few years, particularly in the case of the use of bouncers. For long periods in the 1980s and 1990s, bouncers were unheard of at one-day level. They were against the rules. Bowlers did not want to give away a no-ball for bowling one, so they were put on the shelf. But in the past year or so, bouncers have become a fundamental attacking weapon in the one-day fast bowler's armoury. In fact, the balance was moving so far towards batsmen, that in Australian domestic one-day cricket – the Mercantile Mutual competition – the rules have been changed to allow one bouncer per over. This has been a godsend for bowlers struggling to contain batsmen who, in the knowledge that they won't be facing any short balls, can comfortably move onto the front foot before the ball is released.

Now it is more of a guessing game and a truer test of the ability of the players. It has also brought back some of the most exciting elements of cricket. There are few more exciting and spectacular challenges than an attacking batsman engaged in a battle for domination with a fiery fast bowler who is prepared to bang it in short. The deep fieldsmen behind the wicket – third man and fine leg – are more likely to get catches as the ball is hit in the air more and the exciting shots such as hooks and upper-cuts over the slips come back into the game.

I have no doubt that this shift in the Mercantile Mutual competition has been a positive step and offers great potential at international level, too. The bowler benefits because he has another attacking weapon up his sleeve, as well as a means to keep the runs down if he bowls a decent bouncer over the batsman. And the batsman benefits, too, because a good back-foot player will take full advantage of a bouncer that isn't absolutely on-line. On a general note, more fours and sixes and more spectacular outfield catches will arise from the re-introduction of the bouncer.

A genuine fast bowler's greatest attribute is his pace and his ability to get batsmen out because of it. In the 1998/99 summer, Glenn McGrath decided to use his pace Test-cricket style to unsettle the Sri Lankan batsmen. The strategy worked well and there is no reason it wouldn't work at all levels of one-day cricket. We knew that the Sri Lankans like the ball coming on at good pace, which suits their big hitting in the early overs when the ball is hard and the field is up. But we thought they would be less comfortable against a genuine short assault that meant they could not comfortably plump onto the front foot and belt the ball away through the field.

The Sri Lankan team has such natural clean hitters that any strategy to restrict that attacking approach is a winner. But McGrath did more than that – he exposed a weakness in their make-up that is likely to be followed around the world. The Sri Lankans are so used to the ball being below hip height that their weight and balance generally goes forward automatically as they attempt to exploit one-day bowlers who work on maintaining a straight line and length.

McGrath identified that trait and to counter it, bowled the odd bouncer to rattle the batsmen. He knew he was likely to concede a no-ball or two but was prepared to do so if it meant forcing the batsmen into two minds.

It certainly did in Adelaide during the Australia Day weekend match in 1999. Bowling as if it was a Test match, McGrath intimidated the Sri Lankans with his aggressive tactics that saw them plummet to 6–53 and then succumb for 190 in the chase for our total of 270.

They had scored 303 against England the day before, so we knew how dangerous they could be at the batsman-friendly Adelaide Oval. But McGrath's assault was too much for them, even though he gave up six no-balls on his way to a superb haul of 5–40. The result demonstrated the value of the clear planning and precise execution that went into his effort.

McGrath's tactics had Sri Lanka in a quandary. They lost some of their focus in their approach to batting and they started to play shots they did not need to play. It was another example of the powerful use of an attacking tool that the opposition was slow to respond to.

The batsmen knew that and so they walked out to start their innings with negative thoughts in their minds. They were aware they might face a bouncer or two at any moment and it meant they could no longer comfortably lunge forward as they had done successfully for years. McGrath had won a small victory before he had bowled a ball – and any victories against the Sri Lankan dashers are gratefully accepted. Mind you, that tactic will be less successful in the subcontinent where there is significantly less bounce in the pitches. But on bouncy tracks such as Perth and Brisbane, and in the West Indies, too, it is a prime example of using the conditions and natural attributes to gain an advantage over the opposition.

There is no reason that young fast bowlers can't apply the same strategy to their one-day matches. Bouncers need to be used sparingly because the surprise element will be lost if they are a regular occurrence. But don't be surprised if smart young quicks don't start to exploit the same thing that McGrath did so well.

**Glenn McGrath**
Born 2/2/70
99 matches 891.3 overs 93 maidens 3606 runs 144 wickets
25.04 average 5–15 best bowling 37.1 strike rate
4.0 runs per over

Australia used the same tactic against South Africa in the one-day finals in 1997/98. In that series, South Africa used Daryll Cullinan as an opener – both to use his good hitting skills to get them off to a quick start and also to keep him away from the legspin of Shane Warne for as long as possible. Cullinan's problems with Warne are well known around the world.

In fact, Warne once made the comment that, and there would be few who disagree with his analysis, he

106

would like to bowl to Cullinan for a living. The South Africans knew Cullinan was vulnerable batting at No. 4 if he came out and had to face Warne immediately. But they had no doubt Cullinan was a quality batsman who, if he had a few runs and overs under his belt, would be better equipped to attack the leggie. Anyway, we thought we had an edge on Cullinan and we didn't want to lose it just because he would come in to face the new ball.

The plan was for whichever bowler delivered the first ball to Cullinan in the first final in Melbourne to give him a bouncer directly at the throat. The idea was to let him know that if he was going to come out and slog the new ball because he couldn't play spin all that well, he was not going to get much in his hitting arc. And there would be a surprise in store for him as well.

Steve Waugh knew how well that sort of surprise attack would work. More than a decade ago in a Test match in Brisbane in 1988 against the the mighty West Indies, Australia's tactic was to bounce their captain Viv Richards as soon as he came to the crease. It had a dual purpose – first, the Australians hoped to force a bad shot that would lead to Richards's downfall, but just as importantly, it spelt out a plain message to the West Indian master blaster that no matter his reputation and ability, the Australians were not impressed by his seeming invincibility and were prepared to give him plenty of heat. As it happened, Waugh was the player with the ball when Richards arrived. Despite his tender years and novice standing compared to the great man, Waugh didn't hesitate to apply the plan to the letter. One bouncer. Two. Three. At first amused, then curious, then angry, Richards could do little but accept the bowling from the provocative medium-pacer. If he was intimidated, however, he didn't stay that way for long – he smashed 68 in about as many balls ...

The opportunity in 1997/98 in Melbourne fell to Paul Wilson, the big South Australian quickie who fancies himself as a steaming, snorting speed merchant in the tradition of Merv Hughes and Dennis Lillee. If big Blocker's first delivery was called a no-ball, so be it. There was also the odd chance that if it didn't get too high, but surprised Cullinan, we had a chance to get him out. The plan worked perfectly. Almost.

Wilson banged it in short and Cullinan got into a tangle as he tried to play an awkward pull but instead, only managed to lob it to square leg. Unfortunately, Michael Bevan, who is normally as reliable as any fieldsman in the world, couldn't get his hands on the skier and Cullinan survived.

Bouncers have never been used to greater effect than in the famous clash between Lillee and Richards in the game that is now known as Western Australia's 'miracle match'. Lillee was famous for his aggression, but of all the thousands of bouncers he bowled in his 20-odd years in the game, there can be few more famous than the series he bowled in the most influential one-day over of his career. It happened back in March 1977, when WA beat Queensland in a Gillette Cup semi-final to set up its third trophy success in its most hard-fought one-day campaign. Lillee knew he had to put his stamp on the game immediately given that WA had been bowled out for a paltry 77 and he did so at the start of Queensland's run chase.

Richards, who was playing for Queensland that season, opened and Lillee responded to the challenge by bowling four consecutive bouncers. That wasn't a bad start. The mighty West Indian is probably the best one-day batsman ever to play the game and here was Lillee serving it up to him at express pace. Richards must have had a flashback when Waugh bowled him the welcome-to-the-crease bouncers all those years later. He could hardly have expected Lillee to bowl him two bouncers, let alone three. But after the fourth, he must have thought Lillee was just going to keep bowling them. Instead, the wily Lillee sent down a much slower ball that Richards barely kept out as he suddenly groped forward like a man looking for a light switch in the dark. Next ball, Lillee bowled a superb off-cutter that shattered the stumps to get WA off to the perfect start. Then he put the icing on the cake a few overs later by trapping Greg Chappell caught down the leg-side by Rod Marsh attempting to hook another bouncer. I have always wondered how Richards's concentration was affected by those four fiery bouncers and whether that show of bravado by Lillee had its desired influence on the whole Queensland line-up. They were knocked over for just 62 so I suspect it might have. If it did, it meant Lillee had succeeded in using his greatest attribute – his extreme pace – to gain a major advantage over the Queenslanders.

**Dennis Lillee**
Born 18/7/49
63 matches 598.5 overs 87 maidens 2145 runs 103 wickets
20.83 average 5–34 best bowling 34.88 strike rate
3.58 runs per over

It is an unusual match in which a fast bowler will go for the throat like that. Often, a bowler like McGrath will weigh up the conditions, the pitch and the opposition, realise he is not going to get much reward if he is too aggressive and will throttle back a notch or two. In that situation, he will say to himself: 'Right. I am just going to bowl straight, hit the splice hard and force the batsmen to take chances. I will still bowl quick but my aim is to give away nothing and build pressure by preventing them from scoring.' The overtly aggressive approach will work sometimes but taking the initiative like that and going for the throat, both literally and figuratively, in a bid to break the game open does not happen often.

Such an approach rarely works in one-day cricket unless you have a superb strike bowler such as McGrath or Waqar. Nonetheless, it is worth considering in circumstances when the batsmen are on top, and the medium-pacers look unlikely to break through. Bowlers need to be prepared to try different things because predictability simply plays into the hands of the batsmen.

# Spinners

For many years, spinners were frozen out of one-day cricket – the conventional thinking was that medium-pacers should dominate bowling attacks. Spin bowlers were seen as being too risky and too expensive. They could not produce the run-saving stability of a line-up of five or more solid mediums. Luckily, nowadays that thinking no longer applies, and good spin bowlers play as much of a part in one-day cricket as any fast bowler or seamer. The reason is quite simple – good spin bowlers can be match-winners. A bowler capable of taking two or three wickets in a short burst is a valuable commodity – no matter if he bowls fast, slow or anywhere in between. Shane Warne is the classic example.

Only a handful of one-day players take wickets at a better rate than one and a half per match. In fact, only four one-day players in the history of the game have ever achieved two wickets per match and they played just a handful of games between them. Indian leg-spinner, Bhagwat Chandrasekhar, took three wickets in his sole game; Australian Anthony Stuart got eight in three games, including a hat-trick; West Indies paceman, Ottis Gibson, took 34 in his 15 matches; and mercurial Australian all-rounder Gary Gilmour, took 6–14 on debut in the 1975 World Cup semi-final. He followed it up with 5–48 during the final, and finished his career with 16 wickets from five games.

Dennis Lillee – the best ever? With his pace, aggression and stamina, he constantly maintained a dynamic approach in Test and one-day cricket.

Dean Jones. His aggressive approach to batting, running between the wickets and fielding took one-day cricket to a new level.

Viv Richards in typical fashion – punishing yet another hapless bowler. He is regarded by many as the best batsman of the modern era.

Jeff Dujon is one of my favourite cricketers. I loved his athleticism and excitement behind the stumps. He was also a valuable contributor with the bat.

Colin Croft was a key member of the powerful West Indian pace attack. Although, like his teammates, he wasn't keen on the 'strawberry mousse' uniform used in World Series Cricket.

Mike Gatting might have been a bit ambitious in the 1987 World Cup final with this reverse sweep, but it is now a common feature of one-day cricket. The ball, out of picture, went straight up and was comfortably taken by Australian wicketkeeper, Greg Dyer.

Javed Miandad – busy as a bee. The Pakistani was a wonderful worker of the ball in one-day cricket. His continual turning over of the strike annoyed the opposition and often gave him the upper hand.

Allan Border was a rock-solid member of Australia's middle order in 273 one-day matches. Although he scored just three centuries, he was superb at maintaining the momentum in run chases.

Finesse and elegance personified, Michael Bevan has the highest one-day average ever. He displays a combination of a fine touch and a great mind that constantly assesses what is required by the team.

Part of two successful World Cup campaigns, Tom Moody's experience and versatility makes him a valuable member of any team.

Custom-made. Searching for a shot to relieve pressure in tight situations, Steve Waugh started to 'slog-sweep' the slow bowlers. He used this to great effect in the 1999 World Cup in England.

Two all-time greats: Sachin Tendulkar, often referred to as the closest in style to Bradman, is watched by the world's most successful wicketkeeper, Ian Healy.

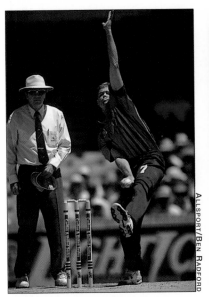

Shaun Pollock's attacking batting and near-perfect bowling make him the one-day game's premier all-rounder.

Sanath Jayasuriya changed the nature of one-day cricket singlehandedly in 1996. His ultra-aggressive approach made the whole world rethink its tactics.

The human rubber ball. Nothing is safe if hit in the air near Jonty Rhodes. He has set the standard for fielding for many years.

A highlight of my career has been the chance to open the batting with Mark Waugh. He is a brilliant player who has proven a great success at both forms of the game.

Wasim Akram – lively, lightning-fast and lethal. He was as quick as anyone at his peak, and can move the ball both ways off the pitch or in the air.

You can't beat that winning feeling. I almost jumped out of my skin after completing the run-out that gave us the series victory over South Africa at the SCG in 1998.

Australia Day celebrations. My first century for Australia came in my second innings after being promoted to open against South Africa in the second final at the SCG in 1998. Thanks Tugga!

As good as it gets. The ultimate prize in one-day cricket – the World Cup. A huge thrill to be part of it and a wonderful moment to share with great teammates.

|                      | Wickets | Matches | Wickets per match |
|----------------------|---------|---------|-------------------|
| Saqlain Mushtaq      | 204     | 108     | 1.88              |
| Waqar Younis         | 285     | 173     | 1.64              |
| Dennis Lillee        | 103     | 63      | 1.63              |
| Shane Warne          | 208     | 130     | 1.60              |
| *Other spinners*     |         |         |                   |
| Muttiah Muralitharan | 163     | 120     | 1.35              |
| Anil Kumble          | 235     | 178     | 1.32              |
| Abdul Qadir          | 132     | 104     | 1.26              |

So you can see how difficult it is for any player to take wickets consistently in the frenetic environment of one-day cricket. Warne is arguably the best leg-spinner the game has ever seen. Whether it is one-day, four-day or five-day cricket, good batsmen struggle against him. He is a prime example of a player whose sheer quality means he can be as effective in the short version as in the longer types of cricket. So, too, Michael Bevan, the left-arm wrist spinner who can be unplayable on a helpful pitch and when his rhythm is good. Both players are hard to negotiate even if the batsman is just trying to keep them out and not score runs — they have a spinner's strongest weapons: the ability to get turn and bounce.

Warne has greater control than other spinners, but his swerve in the air and turn off the pitch makes him a tricky customer in one-day cricket. Bevan generates great rotation on the ball because of his whippy action that helps him bowl at virtually medium pace.

Derek Underwood, Bishen Bedi, Roger Harper and Mushtaq Ahmed are all spin bowlers who have had considerable influence on one-day cricket and who have won important matches for their countries. The Indian master Bedi, in fact, returned some of the most extraordinary figures ever seen in one-day cricket when he took 1–6 off the maximum 12 overs against East Africa at Leeds in the 1975 inaugural World Cup. Needless to say, India won the match comfortably ...

While Warne is a rare example, many teams will have a talented bowler who has a considerable influence on the team's results. There is certainly no rule that says the best bowler in the team has to be a quick.

Many teams right down to junior level will find their best bowler is a leg-spinner or an off-spinner. They can play a role as important as the players who take the new ball. There is certainly no reason why a young leg-spinner should not get a bowl simply because of the type of delivery he produces. Give players an opportunity and both they and the team will benefit.

As one-day cricket evolves, spinners have started to exert more influence than ever before. International teams certainly like to have as much variety in their attacks as they can muster. Every captain wants to be flexible and call on different types of players depending on the circumstances. If two batsmen are set on a good pitch and are playing the medium-pacers comfortably, the option of an attacking leg-spinner could be a match-winner. Or if the pitch is a bit slow, or perhaps it may produce sharp bounce, why not open with an off-spinner whose reduced pace makes it difficult for the batsmen to play their shots against the new ball.

Normally, spinners will be used in the period between the 15th and 40th overs. After 15 overs, fieldsmen can be sent outside the circles to protect the boundaries. This allows the bowlers to mount pressure on the batsmen by drying up their run flow. Many batsmen will look to attack the spinners, but their options might be limited if the bowler can bowl to the field. The role of the spinners, then, is to create wicket opportunities and limit the batting options. If they can make the batsmen concentrate on survival for a while rather than attack, it has been a successful move to bring on the slower bowlers.

Like other forms of bowling, wicket opportunites are created by restricting the run flow. Spinners will make subtle changes to their approach to maintain the pressure. They will tend, for example, not to bowl by floating the ball up in a bid to tempt a lofted shot. Rather, the key will be to bowl on the spot, giving little away and forcing the batsman to make the play. This was evident in the 1996 World Cup final in Lahore where Sri Lanka used a squadron of slow bowlers to strangle Australia's attempts to get a decent total on the board.

By using bowlers such as Muralitharan, Kumara Dharmasena, Aravinda De Silva and Jayasuriya on the slow pitch at the Gaddafi Stadium, Sri Lanka built pressure by attrition – they restricted the run flow and eventually the frustrated Australian batsmen holed out as they tried to overcome their inertia by going on the attack.

Warne, for example, bowls quicker in one-dayers than he does in longer matches. This makes it harder for batsmen to get to the pitch and play attacking shots. But he still is aware of how crucial changes of pace are, so he will vary his tempo considerably during a spell. He doesn't bowl darts either, which was the trend for spinners for years. He still makes it hard to score. When Warne is bowling, the fieldsmen are intensely aware that he is likely to get a wicket any ball, no matter what the state of play and how good the batsmen may be looking. You know the batsmen are looking to be aggressive and positive, which increases the chances of a wicket – and with his changes of pace and line, Warne is always a chance to tempt a poor shot. The batsman is quite likely to come down the wicket and miss, or knock one up in air because he has been deceived by flight.

Warne has proved to be quite an attacking bowler who, surprisingly, may not bowl many leg breaks. In the Pepsi final in India in 1998, Warne bowled only one or two leg breaks in his ten overs. He mostly bowled top-spinners, wrong 'uns and flippers. He is not a big bowler of wrong 'uns, so obviously the pitch was flat and offering so little turn that he put away his stock ball – the big turning leg break – to vary things with subtle changes of pace and bounce.

Spinners will also come into the game if the top order gets off to a flyer in the early overs. By flyer, I mean they are scoring at better than a run a ball and may have a score like 0–60 off eight or nine overs. The batsmen are clearly building a foundation of a very big score and the fielding team needs to shake that foundation a bit or things will get away from them. Warne is used in this role quite regularly. It will be his job to slow the scoring rate, preferably by taking a wicket.

He did this in Barbados in 1999 when the West Indian openers Ridley Jacobs and Sherwin Campbell had flayed us for 81 off 12 overs before Warne came on and stopped the runs with the wickets of both players. This was significant because it slowed the run rate enough for us to restrict the Caribbean cavaliers to 249 off their 50 overs – about 30 runs short of a winning total.

Being the player Warne is, the batsmen are automatically wary when he comes on and will usually reduce their risk-taking, even though he must have two close catchers in position until the 15th over and can only have the two men deep. Despite these restrictions, Warne regularly takes wickets in the early overs. He is a special case though, and the captain has to have great confidence to go to the leg-spinner so early. The captain must be confident his bowler can bowl to the field. The same principle can apply at any level of the game.

Sometimes, the batsmen are hitting the medium-pacers so easily that a dramatic change of pace is required to slow the onslaught. This is where the spinner can be invaluable – as long as he can bowl with reasonable control. As I have noted earlier, the key to bowling in one-day cricket is the ability to hit the right spot ball after ball.

Things are no different for spinners, so they must work hard on their control and their ability to bowl line and length – even if batsmen are charging at them and trying to hit them around the ground. Although it is annoying at training when batsmen try to constantly hit you out of the nets, this can be a valuable learning tool. It is little different from the match situation, except that batsmen are invariably less conservative in the nets because their innings can't be terminated no matter how many times they get out.

Concentrate on bowling to the line and length you consider necessary to combat the onslaught. If you are a leg-spinner bowling to a right-hander, work away on middle- and leg-stumps on a good length.

If you are an off-spinner, aim at off-stump or take your line slightly outside off if it is turning or the batsmen are picking you off through the leg-side. Keep working at bowling straight and full, no matter how many times the ball goes flying back over your head.

You can set a field to that line and length – it is only when you are short or wide that the batsmen start to have free swings. Remember, you only have to hit the stumps once in the batsman's innings during the match to win the battle. It is even better practice if you simulate match conditions when you go into the nets by having a picture in your mind of where your fieldmen are placed. Let the batsman know so that he can try to practise hitting away from the field. Sure, you will have arguments about big hits that he says landed out of reach and you are convinced went down the throat of your deep fieldsmen. That is part of the fun, but it is also important in teaching you where to set your fieldsmen. Practise well and practise as you play and you will play better.

It is important to learn to keep your cool when the batsmen are attacking you. This is easier to do if you have the work under your belt to allow you to continue to bowl straight no matter how much the bats are swinging.

Let's take a look at a couple of other prominent Australian spinners. Bevan qualifies as an all-rounder, despite being in the team as a specialist batsman. His batting in the one-day arena is second to none, yet his freakish skills with the ball make him one of the most exciting players ever to grace a one-day match. Yet he is not the sort of player who will bowl in every match – in fact, he only bowled 18 overs in nine matches in Australia in 1998/99. Nonetheless, he is the sort of bowler who can turn a match. Some days, he lands the ball on the right spot from ball one and you know he is going to have a great spell. He will more than likely bowl ten overs and pick up two or three wickets. Others days, he goes for ten off his first over and he may only get one or two more overs.

Bevan is a spinner who more likely will be used as an attacking option – if the batsmen are getting a few runs or a wicket is needed to break though, he is likely to be thrown the ball. Several times last summer he was the sixth or seventh bowler used. This doesn't mean his being called to the crease was a desperate measure – it was more an indication of Australia's depth of bowlers and the fact that the captain can try many options until he finds one that works on the day. Bevan is less likely to be used as a containing bowler – although his variety and bounce makes him a dangerous proposition, he can be expensive. Bevan works hard on his bowling, but he doesn't enter every game thinking that he is a certainty to bowl.

Another attacking spin bowler is Brad Young, the South Australian who was in the World Cup preliminary squad. He also happens to hold a place in cricket history by being the first and perhaps only bowler to take a hat-trick in a Commonwealth Games match. Young is a left-arm orthodox spinner who takes wickets because he gets good flight and drift but, most importantly, turns the ball. Unlike a lot of finger spinners, he is able to get turn even from unresponsive pitches. That is a valuable commodity because he is able to maintain pressure throughout his spell and constantly probe for wickets. His variation is good and he has a decent arm ball, so he is a fine role model for young left-armers.

# The Slower Ball

Australia won the 1987 World Cup in India and Pakistan with a team of solid batsmen and good allround bowlers who adjusted well to the conditions. But what stood out most from that series, and which is probably the trademark of one-day cricket now, was the arrival of the cleverly disguised slow ball. Bowlers have always varied the speed of their deliveries in a bid to keep batsmen guessing and therefore play false shots. Way back last century, Fred Spofforth, Australia's demon fast bowler, used to bowl a slower delivery by holding just half the ball. It meant he could bowl with the same action but because his hand was not fully behind the ball, it was not propelled at full force. It was effective and helped Spofforth to dominate international cricket in his day.

But it is only in the last decade or so that the definitive slower ball – the one so well disguised that it cannot be picked before delivery – has been introduced and has had such a marked effect on the game. The introduction of slow-motion replays and video recorders has helped, of course. Video enables young players to have an immediate visual reference to show them the various versions of slow balls that bowlers have introduced. It has also forced bowlers to disguise their slow ball, because they know batsmen will be analysing the vision to try to gain an advantage.

Steve Waugh and Simon O'Donnell introduced the slower ball to one-day cricket in 1987; their legacy is an innovation now widespread in the game. Previously, fast or medium-pace bowlers would rarely have a slow ball in their repertoire.

Waugh knew he was onto something before that tournament when he was bowling in the nets at New South Wales team practice. He had been fiddling around with his invention – a ball delivered with the same action as normal but released from the back of the hand so that it looped slowly rather than carried through at its normal pace. One day, Greg Matthews was the guinea pig in pads who had the task of trying to keep out the Waugh invention.

Matthews, who played 59 one-dayers for Australia (mostly in the mid 1980s), was a player not shy of trying odd things nor a man of reserved opinions. Yet he goggled in amazement when he saw what Waugh was trying to do! 'Wow, man,' the excitable Matthews said to his much younger teammate. 'Tugga, if you can control that ball, you'll take 100 international wickets with it.'

Well, he was right. Waugh has gone on to take 191 one-day wickets for Australia (plus another 88 at Test level) making him one of the dozen most successful bowlers the one-day game has ever seen. That was the first time the cricket world had seen a really good slower ball and partly explains why he was so effective. If players had never seen it before, it was going to take them some time to adjust and form defences against it. Until that time, bowlers had used off-cutters or leg-spinners, but this was the first time a bowler had demonstrated the ability to produce a comprehensive change of pace.

Waugh was the Iceman in that World Cup – his control was so good that Allan Border invariably threw him the ball to bowl the last few overs when the batsmen were thrashing at everything. He was only 22 but he took 11 wickets in that tournament at just four runs an over. He bowled the last or second-last over in three matches that Australia won in incredibly close finishes. Against India in Madras, the home team needed four off the over but managed only two and lost by a solitary run. Then New Zealand lost by five runs at Indore after needing nine to win. Waugh bowled Martin Crowe and Ian Smith, scrambled to force a run-out and gave up only three singles in the last over of that match.

Then in the final, England needed 15 off the last four overs with wickets in hand but Waugh's cool head and straight line coupled with a series of slower balls prevented them getting closer than seven runs. Most importantly, he was able to bowl slower balls that the batsmen could not pick – or hit.

For a bowler to succeed in one-day cricket, it is vital for him to be able to bowl a good slower ball. There is nothing more effective, particularly in the death overs, to keep the batsman from scoring heavily.

The reason is quite simple. If a batsman is expecting the ball to come at him at 130 kilometres per hour, and he has swung his bat back above the stumps as he prepares to play a shot as hard as he can, he is in no position to react to a delivery that floats in 50 kilometres per hour slower than expected. That is why you will see batsman suddenly jamming down on the ball as they realise it is not going to arrive in time and they have to adjust their shot just to keep it out. It is very hard to change the momentum of the swinging arc.

Two or three slower balls will often be bowled in the last over or two of the innings as batsman and bowler play a game of cat and mouse with each other. The bowler knows his opponent wants to hit every ball; the batsman knows many of the deliveries he gets will be slow floaters. If the batsman picks the slower ball, he will be able to slog it away. But on the other hand, if he decides to play a premeditated shot thinking it is going to be a slower one, and it whistles through at full pace, he will be lucky to survive, let alone score from it.

The pressure is on the bowler, too. He knows he has to keep the batsman quiet, but he doesn't want to give him a free hit. That means the timing of the slow ball is important. If the batsmen can read when the bowler is going to deliver a slow one – either by body language, change in action or the bowler's history of resorting to it in a certain situation – he will sit back and be able to hit it away over the infield. That's where the bowler has to analyse the situation. He has to read what the batsman is thinking. If the bowler thinks the batsman is coming at him, he doesn't want to serve it up to him. The surprise element is very important.

Others have worked on the slow ball and have mastered it very quickly. Victorian and Australian all-rounder Simon O'Donnell was very good at it. He was not genuinely quick, but he often opened the bowling and soon found he had to master variation if he was to succeed at international level. O'Donnell played in that World Cup in 1987 and it was no surprise that he and Waugh developed the concept at the same time.

Quick bowler Craig McDermott was also one of the most effective slow-ball bowlers I have seen. He disguised it perfectly. McDermott used to charge in with a long, powerful run before whipping his arm over in an explosion of force. But if anything in his action changed to accommodate a slower ball, the batsman would have spotted it in an instant. Instead, and as the result of many hours hard work, McDermott bowled without changing his action or run-up but was able to control the ball so it floated out of his hand.

Merv Hughes, McDermott's partner for many seasons, bowled an effective leg-spinner that while easy to spot, still took a bit of effort to be played. The trouble with his slower ball was that after it had been bowled a few times, the word was out on the international grapevine and batsmen knew to look for it. He countered by bowling it very sparingly in a bid to catch the batsman by surprise. It worked too, with Hughes getting England opener Chris Broad in a Test at Headingley in 1989 as the left-hander played all around a loopy leggie that bowled him. England medium-pacers like Adam Hollioake and Mark Ealham have also developed the slow ball as a part of their strategy. This has helped them step up to play one-day internationals.

Victoria's Ian Harvey is another who bowls the slower ball well. It makes him a bowler the captain is confident of using in the last few overs, and may just get him selection ahead of a similar player if the selectors are looking for the player with a tiny advantage. Any medium-pacer or quick bowler who can't bowl a slower ball is of limited effectiveness in one-day cricket. It is worth working on because the rewards that come from bowling it well will be apparent.

One mistake some players make is to bowl a slow ball by simply letting it fall out of their hand at delivery. These bowlers are aware that by changing their run-up or action, they will telegraph their intentions. So they get into the delivery stride and simply let the ball drop. That may work sometimes, but it is ineffective in the long run. For a start, a good follow-through is essential for a quick bowler to maintain his balance and avoid injury. Pulling up short in the action, which you have to do if you want to just let the ball fall out of the hand, rather than be propelled, puts enormous strain on the back and shoulders. It's like trying to stop a speeding car – you have to slow down over a distance, not pull up on the spot at which you reach your greatest speed. The ball falling can be avoided if you try the following methods to bowl a slow one.

This is the ball perfected by Steve Waugh and the most effective of all slow balls. The advantage is that it comes out significantly more slowly than the other variations, so it has the most dramatic effect on the batsman.

To bowl it well takes many hours of practice, but the rewards will come if you plug away at it. It is effectively a wrong 'un, though it does not have as much spin as an orthodox leg-spinner would impart. And as the bowler is not trying to turn the ball, it is easier to disguise because he does not have to change his wrist position too much.

Hold the ball as for a normal delivery but at the moment of release, the hand rolls over the front of the ball which comes out over the top of the little finger. The back of the bowling hand will be facing towards the gully when the ball is released. It will loop out of the hand and drop suddenly – because it has so little momentum.

122

# Split finger

This is often used by baseballers who want to disguise their change-down ball. You can bowl it with a normal action but instead of having your fingers running alongside the seam, or across it as you would for a normal swinging or seaming delivery, the fingers are spread wider. At the point of delivery, the ball comes out in the 'V' created by the index and middle fingers. The fingers then slide down on each side of the ball as it is released. Because the fingers are not behind the ball and not providing momentum for it, the ball is projected at much slower speed. This needs quite a lot of practice to perfect and often the ball will sail high and over the keeper while you work at getting the balance right. Don't be discouraged – the ball's natural shape from the hand will be that it seems to be turning into a full toss until its lack of power makes it suddenly drop towards the pitch.

SLOWER DELIVERIES INCLUDE THE BACK OF THE HAND BALL (FAR LEFT), LEG SPINNER (LEFT) AND THE TWO VERSIONS OF THE SPLIT FINGER METHOD (TOP AND RIGHT). FAST AND MEDIUM BOWLERS SHOULD HAVE AT LEAST ONE SLOWER BALL IN THEIR REPERTOIRE.

123

# Palm ball

Some bowlers hold the ball in the palm rather than fingers. The effect of this is to release the ball slightly later than normal so that the bowling action has passed its most dynamic point. The higher the ball is held in the fingers, the more energy is imparted to it by the final flick of the wrist during delivery. Holding it lower in the hand will negate that extra power. It also means the bowler can hold the ball longer and release it later. The danger with this is that if you hold it too long, it will be short. Again that is something that can be avoided by practice.

THE PALM BALL DECEIVES THE BATSMAN BY BEING RELEASED LATE IN THE ACTION.

# Off-spinner

The off-spinner works by transferring the energy of the bowling action into revolutions on the ball. Instead of spearing towards the batsman, the ball will be

A SUCCESSFUL BOWLER WILL BE ABLE TO MIX ORTHODOX DELIVERIES LIKE THIS ONE WITH WELL-DISGUISED SLOWER BALLS.

slightly slower than normal. Hold the ball as for a normal delivery, but at the moment of delivery give the wrist a sharp flick as though turning a key. The ball will travel forward, but will also be spinning so it will take longer to arrive. Another advantage of this ball is that it might also turn off the pitch and beat the batsman that way. The change of pace will be subtle rather than dramatic. This is a good ball to use during the middle overs when the batsmen are playing in more orthodox fashion and not yet swinging at everything. Damien Fleming bowls an off-spinner as his slow ball and has been very effective with it.

So, too, has been Pakistani firebrand, Shoaib Akhtar, who showed at the 1999 World Cup that he had subtlety as well as speed with a delightful slower ball.

## Leg-spinner

The ball Merv Hughes bowled. Use a normal grip but turn the wrist over sharply at delivery as with an orthodox leg-spinner. Again, the ball is held a little longer than a normal delivery so does not have as much momentum. It is the easiest of all slower balls to pick, but the batsman still has to play it and because it is spinning, is likely to move off the pitch.

This combines elements of the back-of-the-hand ball and the split finger grip and is perhaps the hardest slower ball to master. The ball is held as normal but at release, the hand pushes underneath it so that it comes out from the tips of the fingers. The base of the hand will be facing the batsman and will be in front of the ball just before delivery. This action gives it backspin which also means it will keep lower than normal. It is hard to bowl it well because the fingers stop gripping it early in the release and are little more than guides to keep it going in the right direction. But it is effective and will usually skid through lower than normal, making it a dangerous ball to play.

Not all of these variations are suited to all players. Some bowlers feel more comfortable bowling a wrong 'un rather than a split finger ball, or vice versa. Experiment with different grips and work on the ones that you feel that you can bowl. And don't be disheartened if the ball doesn't land on the spot first up. It will take many hours of practice to master control of this type of delivery.

But don't despair. Steve Waugh didn't have perfect control when he started, either. Like you, he had to work at it, and had the odd ball fly over the nets as he did. Stick with it and you will have a powerful card up your sleeve to produce when the batsmen are looking their most dangerous.

**3**

# Wicketkeeping

He's the drummer in the band. The centre of the action. The player who controls the tempo on the field. If you notice him taking spectacular catches or whipping off the bails in a frenzy of action, you know he's having a good game. If you don't notice him at all, he's probably having an even better game. He's the wicketkeeper, the player Ian Healy was referring to when he came up with the 'drummer in the band' line.

Heals was right. He might have thought this of the role he played, but it applies equally to all wicketkeepers from international level down to a budding ten-year-old with oversized pads and gloves that come up to his elbows. The wicketkeeper is in the play from start to finish – he's the only player with a realistic chance of being involved in each of the 300 balls bowled in a one-day innings.

Keeping is a job for an enthusiastic and bubbly bloke. Back in junior days, you are encouraged to talk on the field to keep the team motivated and show the batsmen that you are alert and just can't wait to grab the chance when it comes. Well, the keeper is the player who has to keep that chat

127

going; he's the player who has to cajole his teammates when things are not going so well, and he's the bloke who can lead the celebrations when the wickets are coming. Consider the good keepers in recent times. Players like Rod Marsh, Tim Zoehrer and Ian Healy have one thing in common – they are constantly chirping and supporting and demanding excellence from their teammates.

This is key to the keeper's role. Of all the keepers I have seen, I admire Healy the most. I admire his work ethic and his liveliness on the field. You always get the feeling he is trying to create chances through sheer willpower. His body language on the field is tremendous and he always appears to be in control.

When I was a youngster, West Indian keeper Jeff Dujon was the player I loved to watch. Like most players in the Caribbean, he seemed to thrive on the spectacular. The more difficult the catch or save needed, the more he seemed to enjoy the challenge of pulling it off in the most flamboyant manner. He used to dive around rather than use his feet to get to the ball. This might not have been strictly out of the textbook, but it made tremendous viewing for the spectators.

Personality really shines through when you are keeping. If you drop your head, your teammates and the opposition will know straight away. But if you can keep your head up and act confidently, it is an inspiration to your mates. It is no coincidence that blokes like Dujon and Healy, who are such gritty and proud players, are wicketkeepers. These character traits showed in their batting, too. You could sense how highly they valued their wickets and how determined they were to make the most of their chances at the crease.

Keeping is the one position in a match where personality and character really shows through. Both in the field and at training, you're the centre, the focal point. The ball always comes back through you. Remember that and

WICKETKEEPERS SHOULD HAVE NO HESITATION IN CALLING FOR A HELMET IF CONDITIONS REQUIRE IT.

you are on the way to being a good wicketkeeper. But it is not just catching and stopping ability that makes the wicketkeeper the most valuable fieldsman on the field. When you stand behind the stumps, you have the best view of what is going on. You are in the perfect position to observe if the bowler is moving the ball, or bowling the right line and length. You can also note what the batsman is trying to do – whether he is moving his feet, or playing some deliveries better than others.

This is valuable information that can be used to your team's advantage. A keeper must be alert to what is happening during each ball so that he can provide feedback to the bowler or the captain. Don't wait to be asked to monitor the situation, and make constant assessments. It is part of the make-up of a good wicketkeeper to add tactically to the situation. Keep alert. Try to think ahead. It's a good way of staying in the game.

The keeper becomes very important in setting the angles, whether he is the captain or not. A captain should give the keeper the responsibility to check the angles.

Steve Waugh, even in my first game keeping for Australia, quite often asked me to set the angles. He would place the field but then I had to make sure the angles were spot-on and that there weren't two fieldsmen in a line or that they were too close to each other. This is an example of the teamwork that can exist between the captain and the keeper and other members of the team. Although I was quite new to the team, Steve was happy to take my word that the fieldsmen were in the right spot.

Shane Warne. The name sends shivers through opposition batsmen. And with good reason. Warne has dismissed more than 500 batsmen at international level and is arguably the best leg-spinner the game has ever seen. But if he is hard to bat to, keeping to a bowler who can turn it square one ball, and fire a skidding flipper through at ankle height the next, also takes plenty of getting used to.

How to handle Warne was the big question when I was picked as keeper in December 1997. I think I have answered it reasonably well, but it wasn't always quite so clear-cut. Playing most of my cricket at the WACA where you don't get much of a chance to keep to world-class spinners, it was a challenge for me. I had kept to Shane a few times in the nets on the Ashes tour that year, but not enough to get a proper feel for what he does.

Warne doesn't bowl much in the nets and I had never kept to him in a game and only batted against him once or twice. The first time was a Sheffield Shield match at the WACA in December 1994, when I got 11 and 5 and was bowled by him in the second innings. At one stage, I remember clearly that he bowled a ball I thought was a wide, but it turned so far it nearly got through me.

I also batted against Shane in a one-dayer at the WACA in January 1997 when I got 32 and he took 2–17. I got a few against him that day but you couldn't say I had mastered the master.

I knew I was going to have to learn fast. Keeping on a typically Sydney Cricket Ground turner was a long way from the WACA, and I had plenty of work to do. Although I had batted against him only a couple of times, like everyone else, I had watched him pretty closely.

On the Ashes tour in 1997, I consciously discussed Warne with Ian Healy. Heals was helpful, but he wasn't able to give me any secret advice that would unlock the mystery of keeping to a leggie who could make the ball swerve, spin, skid and jump – sometimes, it seems, almost all at once. He just advised me to stick with the basic things – stay low, get your feet working and keep your eye on the ball. That's all you can really do when you are keeping to any bowler, no matter how difficult they are. If you do the basics well, you can be confident that you will keep well.

When I knew I was going to keep for Australia, my first thought was to keep to Shane as much as I could. After being named in the team, I knew we would have only two or three training sessions in the week to follow so I had to make the most of the chances. He doesn't do much bowling in the nets – Shane has a simple action that doesn't need much tuning and his heavy workload in matches means he doesn't need to do too much extra – but he was happy to work with me. He wanted me to do well, of course. It wouldn't do him or the team much good if I kept as though I was all thumbs and missed an edge or fumbled a stumping chance because I hadn't picked the ball.

We worked in the nets for several sessions with me really just getting used to his action, variety and tempo. There was no batsman, so I could concentrate on learning what he could bowl and how they would come out. Shane went through his repertoire and after each leg-spinner, top-spinner or flipper, we would discuss what he was trying to do, what characterised the delivery and what it was likely to do.

131

After a couple of sessions, I was confident I would be okay because I had seen everything he had to bowl.

However, the one thing that television does not show well — and you can only appreciate this fully by actually batting or keeping to him — is how much Shane gets the ball to drift and drop. Michael Bevan is the same. Both bowlers get the ball to swerve in the air and then drop as though it has hit an invisible wall. This ability is often the reason that batsmen, apart from Sachin Tendulkar and Hansie Cronje who have had success against Shane, are not able to attack him without taking enormous risks. People watching probably wonder why the batsman stays anchored to the crease, fending off ball after ball rather than dancing down the pitch and getting to the ball on the full or half-volley. What the television doesn't show is that movement through the air.

Imagine the batman seeing what looks like a full ball about to land on his off-stump. He can stretch out confidently and prepare to drive it hard through the off-side. Instead, the ball fades in towards leg-stump, drops a step short of driveable length and then spits away towards first slip. That was the ball that got Herschelle Gibbs out in the 1999 World Cup semi-final.

Bevan does not have Warne's control but he is probably an even more awkward prospect because he bowls virtually at medium pace and can get the ball to bounce very steeply. His rapid arm action also makes it difficult to read the delivery out of his hand. Bevan is a left-arm wrist spinner, or chinaman bowler, but his orthodox ball, the one that comes back into the right-handed batsman, doesn't turn very much. However, his wrong 'un, the genuine chinaman delivery that goes away from the right-hander, is deadly.

It varies a lot — he will spin it as little as 5 centimetres or as much as 50 to 60 centimetres on a receptive pitch. Add the bounce, and the fact that he is almost impossible to read out of the hand, and he is a pretty tough package for the batsman ... and the poor old keeper, too.

Since Bevan has nowhere near the control of Warne, he is extra hard to keep to because you have very little time to pick up the flight and trajectory of the ball. They used to say of Jeff Thomson that if he didn't know where the ball was going, what hope did the batsman have? Well, Bevan is just the same. He's not quite as quick, of course, but no one knows if the next ball is going to be on a good length, be a waist-high full toss or an absolute ripsnorter that makes the best international batsman look like a backyard slogger.

On the other hand, that is what makes him such an exciting and dangerous bowler. He has the ability to break open a game with a wicket or two. Even if he goes at five or six runs an over, Bevan is just as likely to bowl an unplayable ball and get the best batsman out. His record shows that he gets out good batsmen. He has taken 32 wickets in the one-dayers, including quality opponents like Pakistan's Aamir Sohail and Inzamam-ul-Haq, Sri Lankan Aravinda De Silva and England batsman, Graham Thorpe. He also picked up my former WA teammate, Murray Goodwin, now playing well for Zimbabwe, in our World Cup match at Lord's.

When I look back at my first summer as Australia's one-day wicketkeeper, my stumping of Shaun Pollock off Bevan in the third final against South Africa in Sydney gives me the most pleasure. Pollock had batted well for 28 and charged at Bevan with the intention of hitting him hard and high back over his head. But the ball was a wrong 'un and it bounced quite high when it passed his bat. I was in a good position and as the ball nestled into my glove, I swung off the bails with Pollock stranded. Howzat!

Technically, it was a good stumping because it had bounced so high and I had to drag it down. But it was

133

especially pleasing because it confirmed in my mind that I was a part of the team and good enough to play at this level. I guess it was the full stop in the answer I had to give when questioned about taking Ian Healy's place in the side.

My hundred in the second final the day before was great from a batting point of view, but the stumping was the most satisfying, mainly because of all the discussion about whether I could do the job. It was an emphatic reply to the critics who thought Healy should have stayed in the team.

Not for one moment am I saying that Heals would have missed the chance. In fact, I am sure he would have pouched it as he did with the 39 stumpings he got in his 168 matches for Australia. But I was given a job to do and it was a very satisfying feeling to complete that job in a crucial situation. I had taken as good a stumping as any over my career and had also proved something to myself.

Steve Waugh always says to think positively and to back yourself. That is sensible and valuable advice, but to actually do it, to achieve something difficult, gives you confidence and the knowledge that you have the capacity to achieve at the level you are. You can't beat it.

# Technique

The actual technique of wicketkeeping is no different in one-day cricket than in other forms of the game. Like most elements of one-day cricket, it is just an extension of the structure of normal cricket. As a batsman would extend a forward defensive shot into a cover drive and then into a typical one-day hit over the infield, a wicketkeeper will maintain the basics and just stretch them to suit the circumstances of the one-day environment.

134

# Physical and mental fitness

What stands out in a one-dayer is the intensity required. This, if anything, makes the job harder even if there is less time spent on the field than in a normal match. You can come off the field after three and a half hours and find you are far more drained than after twice that long in the field during a first-class match. Everything is more intense, there is more action and more rides on every ball.

It is quite feasible that a wicketkeeper will have the ball after every delivery of an innings, so fitness and high concentration levels are vital. The batsmen hit more singles, they play more shots and there is more activity, so you might need to come up to the stumps every ball. That translates to 300 occasions in an innings when you might be in the play. There aren't too many footballers in any code who are in the play that often, yet it is taken for granted that their fitness is far superior to wicketkeepers. It shouldn't be. You need great stamina and aerobic ability to enable you to drive up to the stumps over after over for more than three hours.

Batsmen have to be fit to bat for long periods, and bowlers need good stamina for the explosive spells they have to produce. But no other area of the game requires you to be involved every ball – so wicketkeepers need to be super-fit. If you consider most international and first-class keepers around the world, no matter their shape and size, they have one thing in common: good fitness. It is something they work hard to maintain and an essential requirement for budding keepers eager to make their mark in the sport. International keepers know they can be fit enough to get through 45 overs but if they aren't ready to respond in the last couple of overs when the batsmen are running for everything and the ball is being constantly thrown at the stumps, they cannot be the best value to their team. With stamina and fitness comes mental fitness. If you know you can sprint up to

135

the stumps on the last ball of the innings with the same energy as the first, you have a huge advantage.

Being mentally alert plays a large part in a wicketkeeper's game. He needs to provide feedback constantly and stay alert for things happening in the field. He spends the majority of a game by himself, so keeping focused is important – a keeper who drifts off can cost his team dearly. But it is also important that a keeper relaxes between balls to avoid becoming too tense. There is an art to relaxing, just as there is to most facets of the game. If the slips are in position, you can talk to them and turn on and off a lot easier.

It is harder work staying alert and being ready to respond when there is no one beside you. Try taking a few deep breaths when the ball is dead and let all the tension leave you. Whatever method you use, you have to switch back on again as soon as the bowler turns at the top of his mark.

The last five or ten overs are usually the most hectic and the time you are likely to lose concentration. It is all very well to be thinking about where the fielders should be or where the batsman might hit the next one, but if you are not switched on when the nick comes or the batsman skies one straight up in the air, you will let the team down.

You have to keep reminding yourself to work at each ball. Even though it is one-day cricket and there are so many shots and unorthodox things going on, you need to realise that a genuine outside-edge might come at any stage and you must be ready for it.

## Stance

There is no reason to change your stance from that in a normal match, despite the lack of slips. You will still determine the position in which you stand based on the bounce of the pitch and the speed of the bowlers. Some keepers are tempted to go a bit wider on the off-side to compensate for the lack of slips, but that can leave you vulnerable to balls that go down the leg-side. It is a risk you have to weigh up, though, particularly if the bowler is able to land on a consistent line and you are confident that most balls will travel through to the same area. It's a fine line and something you will feel more comfortable about with experience.

Having said that though, I went a little bit wider sometimes to cover the gap when playing in India. The ball doesn't carry as well there. Even though it comes through at the same pace, you have to stand much closer. But the reason I moved, and even then it was probably only 30 centimetres or so, was more to do with the batsmen than the bowlers. The Indian batsmen, particularly players like Mohammad Azharuddin and Sourav Ganguly, are very wristy and tend to open the face of their bats and run the ball very fine. When I moved across, it was as much to make them think about not playing the shots as it was to catch them. But it didn't make them stop dabbing the ball fine through the slip and gully area.

Some keepers have found the WACA difficult because you have to stand much further back. It takes quite a while to adjust to the different conditions and feel comfortable in the right spot. Even so, just about every keeper around the world would say the WACA is their favourite ground. If it is a traditional bouncy pitch, it is easily the best place to keep because you have so much time to see the ball. When keeping, there is nothing better than the ball coming through at a comfortable height. You can rely on it coming through at a good catchable height at the WACA, not down at your ankles.

Apart from the Pollock dismissal in the Sydney final in January 1997, my best stumping was achieved by standing up to WA medium-pacer, Kade Harvey. The victim was prolific South Australian batsman Jamie Siddons, who makes a habit of getting runs against WA in big matches.

He was right on top in the Mercantile Mutual clash at the WACA in December 1997. We had them reeling at 2–5 but Siddons and Greg Blewett had put on 100 in quick time and our total of 285 looked quite vulnerable on the fast pitch and lightning outfield. Both batsmen were keen to charge Harvey, so I thought I would come up to the stumps to prevent that tactic and force them to try another approach.

Talk about paying off. It could not have worked better if we had practised it for a month. Harvey, who is about as fast as anyone I would stand up to, bowled a leg-side yorker to which Siddons stepped out and tried to hit through cover. He was only a few centimetres outside the line, but he missed the ball and it went into my gloves as clean as a whistle low down outside leg-stump. Immediately, I whipped off the bails and Siddons was on his way. That was one of the few times coming up to the stumps to the quicker bowler created a stumping chance.

Adam Dale is one bowler who would like me to be up at the stumps every time he bowls. This brisk medium-pacer relies on subtle variation and a gun-barrel straight line to restrict the batsman. Having me stand up just adds to the pressure on the batsman, which is what Dale is trying to maintain and build every time he hits the delivery stride.

Against England in particular last summer, Adam was keen to have me up from the first ball to prevent Nick Knight and Alec Stewart running down the pitch at him. Even though I could understand his strategy, I prefer to stand back for

138

a few overs to get a feel for the pace of the pitch and whether the ball is swinging or seaming. Keepers will often come up – but I believe the move is better developed as part of a plan to unsettle a batsman, rather than create a stumping.

If the batsman is dancing down the wicket and charging the mediums, the keeper coming up is an effective way to create pressure and take the attack back to him. In this case, it is a tactical move rather than an attempt to get a leg-side stumping.

The strict interpretation of leg-side wides in one-day cricket makes it difficult for bowlers to fire the ball down the leg-side. Certainly, it is worth trying in a bid to turn the game but more often than not, it may cost runs. Even if a stumping is a rare event, coming up to the stumps can really build pressure on the batsman.

I reckon that I have come up to the stumps four or five times in my one-day career and we have got an lbw decision immediately in that over.

A bowler like Steve Waugh is ideal in that situation. His pace might have dropped off a bit since the days when he occasionally opened the bowling for New South Wales in the 1980s, but he skids the ball and with the keeper standing up, the batsman might feel a bit cramped and more likely to play a shot across the line. Instead of playing an orthodox drive, he might have a nagging fear in his mind that he is going to drag his foot across the line – so he plays a riskier stroke and puts himself at risk of being caught in front. It doesn't work every time but it is a good example of the bowler and keeper working as a team to create a chance.

Some bowlers are less comfortable with the keeper up and tend to lose their line and length as they start to worry about bowling wides and what will happen if they spray one down the leg-side. That's no problem. It's important to communicate with the bowler so you have a plan in place. If he doesn't feel right with the keeper up, don't pursue it. But if the bowler feels okay, and the keeper is confident, coming up to the stumps can be a valuable tool for the team.

It is easy to practise by simply getting into a net with the bowler and telling him to let rip. The technique for standing up is the same for mediums as for spinners. Watch the ball from the delivery stride, through the bowling action, out of the hand, down the pitch and into the gloves. Don't worry about what the batsman is doing — just stick to the oldest coaching advice known to mankind: keep your eye on the ball.

Remember, it is important to watch the bowler's hand so you can pick up any variety. If he has a good slower ball, you know you will have to stay down longer.

I now wear a mouthguard just about every time I come up to the stumps. It is only a small matter but any inconvenience it causes is soon gone while a top edge into the front teeth would take far longer to forget.

# Training

Basics, basics, basics. Get the basics right and everything else will follow. A young wicketkeeper could hardly receive more valuable advice than the words Rod Marsh drummed into me at the Australian Institute of Sport cricket academy in Adelaide. There are no secrets to being a good wicketkeeper. Sure, you need good hands and a keen eye, but the key to success with the gloves on is to work on the basics until they are second nature to you. Then work on them some more. It is hard work but the rewards will come when you effect an effortless stumping or get across in front of first slip to take the low sliding catch that turns a match.

My training sessions tend to concentrate about 80 per cent on wicketkeeping to 20 per cent batting.

140

That might seem quite a high ratio but I feel I am not a natural keeper, so I have to work pretty hard on my technique to maintain my efficiency. Maybe it's because I'm a bit taller than most keepers that it doesn't seem to come as naturally to me. I have always admired a player like Tim Zoehrer for whom keeping comes so naturally. He is very athletic and graceful. His footwork is so precise and his hands so soft and yielding that he is always good to watch.

Here are some of the exercises I do to stay sharp. As Rod Marsh said, do them until you feel comfortable. If that takes 20 minutes, keep at it. If you feel good after two minutes, that's fine. It's all about finding your rhythm. But it is important that you don't just mistake quantity for quality.

I like to set up the drills as close as possible to the match situation – both in conditions and intensity – because that is the best way to learn. You will entrench good habits if you do things right at training that are virtually identical to what you would do in the game.

This also means going outside your comfort zone and really extending yourself. If you catch every ball at training, you are not being tested enough. Instead, work yourself so that you are better than you were. It is only by testing yourself and pushing yourself beyond your present limits that you will get better.

That means you shouldn't be afraid that if you miss a few, you are having a bad session. It may be exactly the opposite. By pushing your limits – either by staying down longer, or getting further across, or taking the ball more cleanly – you are likely to improve and what seems difficult today will be a standard task tomorrow. Remember, don't just practise what you can do well already.

It pays to have your coach have a look at you to see that your footwork is crisp and you are doing things right. If possible, get your coach to videotape you. You can be told a million times what you are doing wrong, but until you see it, and what you have to do to rectify the problem, it may not sink in. Video recorders are probably the best coaching tool of all time because they are 100 per cent objective. You can use video to identify and correct errors in your technique, but it is also very useful in capturing what you are doing right. This means you have a ready reference to come back to if you feel something is going wrong later. It is also a great way of reinforcing correct technique in your mind.

Gloves. I like to mix it up at training by doing some exercises with them on and others, such as short reflex work, just wearing inners. I never use bare hands. Interestingly, Tim Zoehrer was not big on using gloves at training and thought he got a better feel for the ball by using his bare hands. My preference is to use gloves because I like to get as close to the match situation as possible. It's really up to you but remember that your fingers and hands are the tools of your trade, so it pays to be careful.

## Drills

**1.** A good start is a simple catching exercise with a batsman hitting the ball from ten or 15 metres. You control the tempo so you can get into your rhythm. The catches don't have to be too hard – you just want to get your feet moving and get the feel of the ball in your gloves. Ask the batsman to vary the speed and direction so you move side to side and don't take them all at the same pace. It's an easy drill but an effective warm-up. You control the session and move on when you feel things are comfortable.

Remember to have the ball struck over the distance you would experience in the game. You will probably never stand 2 metres behind the stumps in a match, so don't waste valuable training time by catching over that distance.

SIMULATE MATCH CONDITIONS AS MUCH AS POSSIBLE DURING TRAINING DRILLS BY HAVING THE BATSMAN HIT OVER THE DISTANCE YOU WOULD NORMALLY STAND BACK IN A GAME.

**2.** Nicking catches to the keeper and slips cordon is the most common training exercise you will see – and probably the least efficient if it is not done correctly. Unless the batsman is accurate and the thrower can hit the right spot, you spend more time picking balls up than catching them. The biggest problem is that keepers often tend to wander around into a first or second slip position during this drill, simply to get more of the ball. But you don't field there in the match, so it doesn't really help you if you are trying to pick off square cuts rather than the slight edges that come in real life. Make sure the slips are in the right position if you are going to do this.

I find it far more efficient to do this exercise alone. Again, you control the tempo. Get the batsman to go down on one knee or get the ball thrown underarm to simulate pitches that keep lower or come up almost onto the bat to take close catches like you would off a spinner.

**WICKETKEEPING**

ONE OF MY PRACTICE EXERCISES USING A TENNIS BALL. NOTE HOW I KEEP MY INNERS ON EVEN FOR THIS SOFT BALL DRILL. A WICKETKEEPER'S HANDS AND FINGERS ARE THE TOOLS OF HIS TRADE, SO IT PAYS TO LOOK AFTER THEM.

Another tip – try to use balls that are reasonably hard, not the soft rubbishy balls that seem to come to the end of their working lives by being used in slips practice. Match balls tend to be hard, so make sure you use something as close to the real thing as possible. It seems incongruous that you are expected to catch a first-ball nick with a cherry that has a high seam and hard leather but often you have only practised with balls that could be used at Wimbledon.

**3.** Ground fielding. Wicketkeepers do more fielding in one-day matches than other forms of the game so they have to be adept at chasing and throwing. Often the keeper will be the only fieldsman within 15 or 20 metres of the bat so there will be plenty of work to do. Practise throwing at the stumps – and work hard on getting your glove off neatly and quickly. Stand back about 10 metres from the stumps and have someone roll the ball out to you. Do the same going sideways, just as if the batsman had tickled one around the corner and set off for a single. Get down in your crouch then come up and go after the ball as if the batsman had pushed onto the off-side. Practise these as hard as if they were the real thing.

**4.** High balls. Catches off top edges are ever-present in one-dayers, so work hard on running backwards or sideways with your eyes on the ball. Get a batsman to hit the ball directly overhead so you become used to standing under a swirling catch. Practise calling too, so that it comes as second nature in the match.

**5.** Keeping in the nets to a bowler. There is little point in going into a regular net because you can disrupt the batsman, and if he is batting properly, you may not get to glove many balls anyway. But it is valuable to use a shadow batsman – a player who will hit some balls but will mostly deliberately play and miss – when you

CLOSE REFLEX WORK IS A GREAT WAY TO DEVELOP HAND–EYE COORDINATION. ONE-DAY CRICKET REQUIRE SHARP RESPONSES, SO THE BETTER YOUR TRAINING, THE SHARPER YOUR RESPONSES WILL BE.

**WICKETKEEPING**

are working on keeping up to a bowler. The shadow batsman will keep you alert because you don't know how many he will allow to pass but you will get enough balls in the gloves to be able to work on things like watching the ball out of the hand, coming out of the crouch and staying low for as long as possible.

You can also get someone to throw rather than bowl the ball. Work hard on the difficult things, such as going down the leg-side to take full wide deliveries. You can use the full length of the pitch and get the thrower to vary them by throwing at different speeds.

**6.** Short catches almost on the bat are ideal for sharpening reflexes. This is one exercise during which I concentrate on keeping my eye on the ball and staying down for as long as possible. The batsman will use the face of the bat to try to run the ball to the ground and it is your job to just about grab it off the bat itself. It is an intense exercise and does not need to last too long.

CATCHING ALMOST DIRECTLY OFF THE BAT IS AN INTENSE EXERCISE, BUT IT PREPARES YOU FOR THE TOUGH CHANCES THAT WILL COME YOUR WAY.

PRACTISING WITH A GOLF BALL HELPS KEEPERS DEVELOP SOFT HANDS, AND THEY CAN PRACTISE IT VIRTUALLY ANYWHERE, ANY TIME. IAN HEALY SWEARS BY IT.

**7.** Golf ball. Ian Healy is never without a golf ball in his pocket when he is on tour. He religiously finds a wall at the hotel or near the change-rooms and works on his reflexes and hand skills by simply bouncing the ball back off the bricks. This is great for developing soft hands – the mark of the good keeper.

**4**

# Fielding

Fielding is one element of one-day cricket that has indisputably taken the sport to new heights. Many cricketers once saw fielding as little more than a chore between batting and bowling – a boring drag broken up by the occasional task of returning the ball to the bowler as quickly as possible. Now it is acknowledged as one of the most spectacular and influential aspects of the game.

Picture this common sight in a one-day match today. An athletic fieldsman sprints 70 metres at top pace in pursuit of a fully fledged attacking shot. He chases the ball to the boundary. Then, just as it seems that his momentum will force him to crash into the fence, he drops into a slide and flicks his quarry back into the field of play. Leaping to his feet, he picks up the ball then rockets a flat, hard throw straight into the keeper's gloves directly beside the bails. It is a magnificent piece of fielding, as exciting to watch as a stylish cover drive or an attacking over from a fast bowler. Yet this can happen time and again during a one-day innings, as fieldsmen exhibit skills that would be envied by competitors in an

149

Olympic decathlon. Running, jumping, diving, throwing – these activities take place within seconds of each other and are all performed at breakneck speed. No wonder the crowds become so excited and express themselves with such fervour.

The legacy of one-day cricket is that fielding has been taken to new levels in all forms of the game. No matter if it is a Test match or a junior game on a suburban ground, the fielding skills on show will reflect the advances pioneered in one-day cricket. It is now rare that you will see a lumbering fast bowler hiding near the boundary line and hoping the ball won't come near him – it is more likely that he will have the strongest arm in the team and will be placed to take advantage of this skill.

Take Glenn McGrath and Merv Hughes, for example. The power of their throwing arms is well known – they have been responsible for many run-outs because of their ability to throw accurately and quickly from deep in the outfield.

The fielding techniques used in a one-day match can be applied to all forms of cricket. While batsmen and bowlers need to make plenty of adjustments when they move from first-class to one-day cricket, fieldsmen don't change a thing. The skills of chasing, throwing and backing up remain the same, no matter if the players are in a 50-over match or five-day match. The only change is the increased intensity of one-day cricket – the same intensity that has created the remarkable fielding improvements now commonplace.

Now you might be wondering what a wicketkeeper knows about fielding. Well, for a start, the keeper is the player who takes most of the returns and knows how well his teammates are doing at this part of the game. The frenetic nature of one-day cricket means that the keeper will have plenty of work to do in fielding balls, throwing at the stumps and backing up other players when they are able to get to the stumps quicker.

This wicketkeeper actually spent several of his early matches for Australia without pads or gloves on. The experience was enjoyable, but I was grateful for the chance to get behind the stumps.

Every player in a one-day team has to be versatile and be prepared to display skills that might not be their strength. A good example is the 1997 South African tour. Even though I am happier with the gloves on behind the stumps, my first break into the national one-day team meant I had to spend time in the field, rather than keeping.

I couldn't wait to get the gloves on as soon as possible, particularly after I battled to hang onto a couple of catches in my first few matches. I played as the keeper in my first four matches for Australia, but my fifth, at Durban in April 1997, found Ian Healy back behind the stumps and I was required to take on a fielding role. Mark Taylor was out and with Mark Waugh injured, it seemed natural to slot the second wicketkeeper into the slips. My confidence was up. I had scored 77 in Australia's innings after coming in at 4–50. I had also felt good at training after taking slip catches from all directions. Heals asked me if I wanted to field there and I was quick to accept. 'Right,' I thought. 'First slip has to be the easiest position on the field. Tubby Taylor has taken everything that has gone there for more than five years and I reckon I'll just follow his example.' Whoops.

In the space of three overs, I dropped both Adam Bacher and Daryll Cullinan from edges that I must admit were not the hardest catches of all time. Andy Bichel and Adam Dale were the unlucky bowlers and though they didn't say much, they may have looked a tad relieved when I was banished to the outfield. Three days later we moved to Johannesburg and I attracted the attention of the Wanderers crowd when I managed to spill one in the outfield. That seemed to ignite one bloke in the crowd who started to shout out every few minutes as I took up my station at third man.

'Hey, Gilchrist. Where's your vest?' he shouted. I tried to ignore him, but I couldn't help laughing when the punchline eventually arrived after he had yelled the question a few dozen times. 'He doesn't need one,' another wit shouted. 'He couldn't catch a cold.' It was so obvious that I should have seen it coming. About 4000 people in the crowd thought it was pretty funny and had a good laugh. So did I . . . for a moment or two.

Then someone threw a small jar at me. It hit me in the chest and bounced away a few metres. Immediately, another wag yelled out: 'There's another one down', which set the crowd off again. Needless to say, I enjoyed the eventual move behind the stumps, though I did enjoy the stint in the field. And I was able to silence the Wanderers crowd for a few minutes at least when I ran out Derek Crookes with a direct hit from mid-on. Who said keepers can't field?

Players from the 1960s say there was no better fieldsman in the world than the extraordinary South African, Colin Bland. The Eagle, they used to call him. His specialty was patrolling the covers and throwing down the stumps while off-balance from side-on. A decade or so later, Australians Paul Sheahan and Ross Edwards were touted as being among the best. Each of these fieldsmen must have been fantastic players whose skill and dedication placed them head and shoulders above their peers.

Well, the two best fieldsmen in the world today certainly stand out from the rest. But unlike Bland's day, and perhaps that of Sheahan and Edwards too, the gap between them and the pack is getting smaller. Players work so hard at their fielding, even using video recorders to check they are using the correct techniques, that the general skill level has probably never been higher. Even so, I don't think anyone in the world today can match Ricky Ponting or Jonty Rhodes as they stalk the covers like leopards waiting to pounce. These two are superb fieldsmen whose exquisite skills and athleticism bring people through the gates to watch them play. There is certainly an air of excitement in the crowd when either player goes near the ball.

I can't separate them when it comes to deciding which one is the better fieldsman. Rhodes is the better stopper – if anyone in the world has ever been better I'd love to see the videotapes – but no one can match Ponting when it comes to throwing at the stumps. Both are deadly and both are worth dozens of runs to their teams every time they walk onto the field.

Ponting and Rhodes share several attributes – they are short men, just like Don Bradman who was hailed the best fieldsman of his generation, and have low centres of gravity, tremendous foot-speed and lightning reflexes that they work to maintain and improve.

Rhodes is uncanny in his ability to get to the ball, stop it and throw it in almost in the same movement. His great skill is to dive, bounce back onto his feet and release the ball. The way he gets into position to throw the ball is like lightning. Many fieldsmen who dive full-stretch and stop the ball will still give up a single because they cannot release it quickly enough.

Rhodes is explosive in the way he knocks the ball down, gets up as if he was made of rubber, balances and throws it before the batsman is able to get home. This builds pressure on batsmen and forces them to take risks that perhaps they shouldn't take. Like Ross Edwards, Rhodes is a brilliant hockey player who actually represented his country in that sport.

Ponting is not as spectacular as Rhodes in his stopping and releasing, but he is so quick on his feet and so unerring in his aim that he is virtually worth two players in the infield. Time and again, Ponting hits the stumps during a match. And on plenty of those occasions, he catches the batsmen short of their ground.

153

When he ran out the stylish Sri Lankan Marvan Atapattu with a typical swoop and underarm throw at the stumps in Perth in January 1999, he proved that he is deadly when he gets the ball in his hand.

That sort of accuracy plays havoc with the batsmen. They are often not sure whether to run when the ball goes near Ponting, and then get caught in two minds. They will start to hesitate when they are running, leading to mix-ups with their partner and the chance of a run-out. They are also likely to become tentative in their approach and no longer look to score as many runs as they should.

Few things lift a fielding team like a direct-hit run-out or even just a good throw that hits the stumps. It is as if a message has gone through the players: 'We're hot today and we only have to work a bit harder and throw ourselves around a bit and things are going to happen.'

Similarly, there are few things that disconcert the batsmen like the ball whistling into the keeper's gloves above the stumps every time they play a shot into the infield. It is a constant reminder to the batsmen that the fieldsmen are just waiting to pounce and helps to build the psychological pressure. The mere presence of Rhodes or Ponting on the field gives South Africa and Australia the advantage if the batsmen begin to hesitate when the ball goes near them.

## Practise, Practise, Practise

It is no coincidence that Rhodes and Ponting are so good, because they work harder on that part of their game than most other players. As Bland found so many years ago, the only way to perfect the art of hitting the stumps is to do it — hundreds and thousands of times.

After that match in Perth, Ponting explained that he always did an exercise before the start of play that would help him during the game. 'I work hard on direct hits,' he said. 'I do a drill before the game with 20 to 30 throws at the stumps. I always incorporate hitting the stumps in my drills.'

That simple exercise, in which he fields and throws a series of balls hit to him, prepares Ricky Ponting mentally and physically. And it doesn't hurt, either, to hit the timber a few times just before the game starts, particularly if any opposition batsmen are watching.

It is one of the old maxims of cricket that you have to enjoy fielding because you do more of it that anything else. The same applies in one-day cricket. You are in the field for three and a half hours, and as you will rarely bat that long and will only bowl for a fifth of that time at the most, why not work to maximise your enjoyment of fielding.

The intensity of one-day cricket is greater than most forms of cricket, so there is no excuse for getting bored or claiming you are out of the game. Chasing, throwing or backing up – hardly an over goes by in one-day cricket in which each fieldsman is not involved. You will find that fielding is not a chore after all and it may even give you the chance to win a game with a run-out or a timely catch.

Remember, too, that your selection in the team might depend on your fielding skills. If two players are equally matched in batting or bowling, the player who is the better fieldsman will invariably get the nod.

Rhodes might be able to score 40 runs off 40 balls but plenty of other players can do that, too. But when you add that 40 to the 30 runs he will save in the field, he has effectively contributed 70 runs to the team's cause – perhaps enough to win the match and certainly enough to confirm his selection. Any batsman would love to start his innings with 30 runs' credit – which is virtually what Rhodes does.

It is imperative that you work hard at training to improve and hone your fielding skills. Don't dawdle after the ball and then lob it back to the keeper – train as if you are playing in a match.

Former Australian coach, Bob Simpson, was adamant that players had to put themselves under pressure to improve. His idea was that if you trained with match intensity, and trained efficiently and with good technique, you would perform well in a match situation.

That's simply commonsense. Just as a sprinter doesn't improve his speed by doing nothing but jogging, neither does a fieldsman get better by training at half pace. Simpson knew that hard and efficient training made better players, but it also helped the confidence level of players.

The powerful West Indian teams of the mid 1980s were similar. They had many naturally gifted athletes who, like thoroughbred racehorses, benefitted from the hard training they were put through by Clive Lloyd and Viv Richards.

Simpson believed that if you could survive one of his rigorous fielding drills, you could handle anything thrown at you on the field. Geoff Marsh inherited the same beliefs and not just because they worked so well with him. Swampy became one of the best gully fieldsmen the world has ever seen – snaring full-blooded cut shots as a matter of course – but only after spending hours and years working on his skills. Simpson referred to Swampy as 'Iron Hands' when he first came into the Australian team, a reference to the original 'Iron Gloves' Rod Marsh, perhaps, but credited him with working tremendously hard on improving his catching in one of the hardest positions on the field.

# Warming Up

One of the things Simpson introduced was fielding as a warm-up before the start of a match. This has since become mandatory for virtually all senior teams. Players often feel under-prepared if they don't do it. Mind you, there are plenty of players who don't like it. They grumble that if you are going to be out there for three and a half intense hours in a one-day innings, why would you want to do another hour's work on top of that? It is simple. A good warm-up prepares fieldsmen physically by warming the muscles and setting them for the action on field, as well as focusing the mental side of things. If you take a few sharp catches, or hit the stumps in the session, you can take that success into the match. It is just like having a running start in a sprint. If everyone is doing it, you are already behind the field if you don't do it.

And though it might have some tough exercises, the warm-up is not a session with a heavy workload that would drain the fieldsmen of their energy. It is simply a method to heighten awareness, loosen the limbs and even get rid of a few butterflies.

The baseball gloves will often come out at this stage. Former WA coach Daryl Foster introduced gloves at training early in his remarkable 20-year stint with the state team − not to improve catching skills, but as an aid in repetitive throwing exercises. The goal of these exercises was to improve players' throwing skills, not catching, so the gloves were simply handy devices to save time and allow the focus on the primary task.

The training techniques of other sports such as touch footy and soccer are regularly introduced to our sessions. They are good for team morale, hand−eye coordination and fitness − unless you damage a knee as both Dean Jones and I have done.

157

Swimming is also on the training agenda – to boost fitness and help recuperate from injury and weariness. However, there are a few players around who are not all that happy about the pool. Big Carl Rackemann was known for his bustling bowling and amusing fielding, rather than his swimming skills. He also has a keen eye for irony, which is probably why he had this question for Queensland coach, John Buchanan, before a compulsory swimming session. 'Hey John,' he asked. 'Does Kieren Perkins strap on the pads and face a few deliveries in the nets before a big race?' Not surprisingly, Buchanan told him to swim . . . or sink.

# Throwing with Both Hands

Techniques that have changed in recent years, apart from the general improvement in the skills of all players, include sliding, which we will cover later on pages 169–72 and throwing. As techniques evolve further, ambidextrous fieldsmen – players who can throw with both hands – are likely to become more common.

Australian selector Trevor Hohns is one man who says that if he had his time again, he would work on his left-hand throwing. He was a leftie when he batted but a right-hand bowler, so perhaps he was already halfway there.

All fieldsmen practise running in to stop the ball and throw underarm with both hands, but there are not too many players around who can get the ball in from 20 metres or more on both sides. Batsmen regularly take an extra run if it is hit to a deep fieldsman's non-throwing side, so can you imagine the immediate improvement in a fielding team's efficiency if a few outfielders were able to return the ball with equal strength with both hands. I don't think it will be too long before players at international level are demonstrating these sorts of ambidextrous skills.

# Fielding to the Batsman

The adage that bowlers must bowl to the field has been taken to a new level by South Africa. Instead of placing fieldsmen in positions to which the batsmen are likely to hit the ball, South Africa has taken the strategy a step further by placing one man in a position and then bowling so that the batsmen have to hit to him. That man is Jonty Rhodes. This remarkable development in the game may be seen more often in the future as teams exploit the special skills of their players.

In 1997/98, South Africa stationed Rhodes at short midwicket during the middle of the innings and had that wily old fox, Pat Symcox, firing the ball in at leg-stump to the right-handed batsmen. It was a specific ploy and it worked. Symcox was very accurate – managing to get at least 40 deliveries in his 60-ball spell in the right place – and with a bit of bounce and spin, there was nowhere the batsman could hit but through midwicket. Yet there was Rhodes, as agile and fast as ever, to cut off anything but the most full-blooded strokes.

Shaun Pollock and Allan Donald also try the tactic when they have Rhodes at point in the early overs. Both are top-quality bowlers and can maintain a good line and length. They tend to bowl short of a length just on or outside off-stump, pushing the batsmen onto the back-foot and restricting their hitting arc to square on the off-side.

As I mentioned earlier, that strategy led to the run-out of Mark Waugh in our first opening partnership for Australia. It was the result of good thinking and great teamwork from the South Africans. They can get away with it because of the quality of their players and the fact they have played together for many years and know each other's games inside-out.

159

Players on the subcontinent are also improving their fielding, though they don't yet have a Rhodes or Ponting in their ranks. The attitude of Indian and Sri Lankan teams in the past seems to have been: 'Well if we don't save 20 runs, we will just get them when we bat.' Australia tends to go the other way. We think that if we save 20 runs, that's 20 we don't have to score ourselves or 20 the opposition has to find somewhere else.

# The Sub-Fieldsman

Allowing 12 players in Mercantile Mutual matches has been a great innovation to enable specialists to concentrate on their main skill. In WA, big strike bowler Jo Angel is quite happy to allow a more spritely fieldsman on the ground while he puts his size-14 feet up after a spell.

Merv Hughes carried it an extra step during his one-day stint with the Canberra Comets. Merv would bowl his over then swap with a fieldsman who would be on the field for the next six balls before being replaced by Hughes again. That boosted Canberra's fielding strength and allowed Hughes to rest and come back a little more strongly.

The use of the sub-fieldsman has merit and may even be developed further. I don't think it will be too long before specialist fieldsmen are used in international one-day matches to replace bowlers. The spectacle can only improve with a greater number of strong fieldsmen on the ground.

# The Strongest Fieldsmen

The best fieldsmen in the team will invariably be in the circle. They are the players who are required to get direct-hit run-outs or to cut off the ball that would normally go though to the outfield. They are the players who need to create something out of virtually nothing, just as Ponting and Rhodes do so often. They need to have a good throwing arm, though pure strength is not essential. The players with the strongest arms will usually field on the fence where they can get the ball back quickly, though this is not an absolute requirement – I will discuss this later. A poor arm will be exploited by a batting team that will regularly take a run on it. If the fieldsman is strong, taking that extra run becomes a risk.

The captain also needs to be in the circle because he needs to liaise regularly with the bowler and keeper. Steve Waugh sometimes takes up station at short fine leg, or short third man, while Allan Border became one of the most deadly midwickets in the one-day game. He had a rocket-like throwing arm that seemed to home in on the stumps with some form of cricketing radar, and an uncanny ability to take catches from shots that had no right to be caught.

It is important that the midwicket fieldsman has good hands because so many catches go there. Mark Taylor also used to field there and though he was not as quick to throw as Border or Ponting, he had the safest hands in the business. Any player who can snare 56 catches in just 113 one-dayers certainly has sticky fingers – as Taylor has demonstrated time and time again.

Taylor's catching ability even won him a Man of the Match award in his first game as Australian captain. It was in Sydney, December 1992, in a rain-affected clash that both captains wanted to call off because they thought the pitch was unfit for play. The umpires ordered a 30-over match. Australia struggled to 101 with Dean Jones getting a stubborn 21 and Greg Matthews 11 with about as many leg byes. They were to be crucial runs.

Phil Simmons and Curtly Ambrose took three wickets apiece and were almost unplayable at times. When the West Indies batted, Taylor took four catches, including Keith Arthurton who edged one very fine. At slip, Taylor hurled himself to his right to take a superb one-hander.

That sent the Windies to 5–31 before Taylor took the next three catches to set an Australian one-day record and help dismiss the visitors for 87. Paul Reiffel took 3–14 but, rightfully, Taylor received the Man on the Match award for his catching and fluent captaincy that had kept Australia on track to a remarkable win.

Rarely has a player had such an influence on a one-day match without scoring runs or taking wickets, yet he was virtually a unanimous choice as the most influential figure on the ground. And Taylor showed a glint of the steel in his make-up, too, when he interrupted Bob Simpson as he was about to outline the match strategy to simply say: 'Thanks Simmo, I'll take it from here.'

Although fielding skills are improving all the time, there will always be fieldsmen in one-day cricket who are not as fast or as strong as their teammates. They need to be placed where they are likely to see as little action as possible.

That becomes harder every season, though, as batsmen become more adept at hitting to all points of the ground and exploiting weaknesses in the field. The straighter positions such as mid-on and mid-off, or fine leg and third man, are still the best places to put poor arms or slow runners.

Because he is in a straight position, the player doesn't have to make too many sudden lateral movements, but has a bit of time to identify where the ball is going and move into position. There is less need for the agility so vital in the key positions on either side of the pitch where the ball is struck often. Batsmen will quickly ascertain the strength and speed of the fieldsmen and will look to exploit them if they can.

If they know a player is slow over the ground, or has a poor throwing arm, or runs around the ball in the outfield instead of attacking it, he will be picked out. But having less advanced skills will not prevent players from being effective fieldsmen if they can make the most of their abilities. They can work on really attacking the ball in the outfield – charging at it and getting it in as quickly as they can.

Most batsmen will hesitate to run if a player has the ball in hand and is preparing to throw. Just the act of attacking the ball may be enough to stop the batsman taking another run.

And work on throwing. Every training night should include a session of throwing the ball. It is the simplest art in the game yet, like most things, throwing thrives on repetition.

# Underarm Throws

Underarm throws have become much better in recent years, which is not surprising given the number of balls that have to be fielded within a few metres of the bat. As batsmen become expert at taking the pace off the ball and just dropping it at their feet for a quick single, so too have fielding techniques evolved to counter it. In a bid to save time, fieldsmen will often do away with a backswing when they run in and throw at the stumps from just a few metres. They virtually scoop it towards the stumps because the split-second saved by eliminating the backswing (and just relying on the momentum of running in) can be quite significant.

Look at these figures. A person capable of running 100 metres in ten seconds takes one second to cover ten metres, 0.1 seconds to cover 1 metre, 0.01 seconds to cover ten centimetres and 0.001 seconds to cover 1 centimetre. That's one-thousandth of a second to cover 1 centimetre.

Of course, a fully laden batsman is going to take a fair bit longer than world-champion sprinter Maurice Greene, or Trinidadian hero, Ato Boldon, in full flight. The batsman is weighed down with a bat, helmet and pads and he has to back up, stop, accelerate, and prepare to come back for a second run.

Say it takes our batsman four seconds to cover the 17 metres between the creases – meaning he would not quite have reached the halfway point of the 100 metres as Bailey and Bolden are going through the tape. That's a reasonable time given that Dean Jones, the best runner between wickets the one-day game has ever seen, timed himself to take just under ten seconds for three runs and less than three seconds for a single.

Even at that rate, it would still take our batsman just two-thousandths of a second to cover that vital last centimetre. But if a fieldsman can save that much time – a couple of thousandths of a second, or much less time than it takes for a blink of an eyelid – he could do enough to win or lose the match.

How many run-outs do you see referred to the third-umpire in which the bat is just on or just over the line? That is a matter of 1 or 2 centimetres and it has taken the batsmen just a few thousandths of a second to cover it. But if a fieldsman can save that tiny fraction of a second in getting rid of the ball, it could mean the difference between a wicket and a win or a close not out and a loss.

Remember, it is far easier for a fieldsman to cut two-thousandths of a second from his gather and throw than it is for a batsman at full pace to accelerate even further to make up that fraction.

The same applies to throws that hit the stumps or just miss, or balls that the keeper takes above the bails or stretches to reach. How many times do you see the batsman home when the keeper has to stretch to get the ball to the stumps? Sometimes, success is measured in the smallest fractions of time. So, getting rid of the ball as quickly as possible, as well as ensuring your throws are as accurate as possible, can make a huge difference. They are both skills that can be improved with training and can have an enormous impact on your performance and that of your team.

Players such as Ricky Ponting and Jonty Rhodes, the natural infielders, have refined their throws to such a degree that on short balls – say up to 5 metres or so – they hardly use any backswing and simply scoop the ball towards the stumps. They use their foot-speed to create the momentum needed to get the ball in and simply concentrate on picking it up quickly and being accurate with their return. They don't need to produce a hard return if the ball is only going to travel a few metres, so they don't bother wasting time on a backswing. And by minimising the movement of their hands, there is less chance of the return missing the stumps.

This is a skill that Ponting and other players work very hard to perfect. It is an explosive and ever-present element of the game and often develops into a game of cat-and-mouse between batsman and fieldsman.

The fieldsman knows the batsman is just waiting to drop the ball at his feet and scamper through for a quick single. If it only goes a metre or so from the bat, and the cover or midwicket is 15 metres away, it is almost impossible for even the best fieldsman to get close enough to run out either batsman if they are alert and take off immediately.

But the batsman is aware how slight his margin for error is. If he hits the ball a fraction too hard and it rolls 5 metres, not 2, or his partner at the non-striker's end hesitates for even a moment, one of them could easily be run out by a sharp piece of work.

It becomes a fascinating mind game in which the player who is most disciplined and most able to keep his cool is likely to emerge the winner.

# Relay Throw

Relay throws are now very much a part of one-day fielding, particularly on bigger grounds like the WACA and the MCG. This essential development in the game arose from the realisation that two flat, hard throws would get the ball back over the stumps faster than than one looping, long throw. And it certainly adds to the spectacle. It is one of the great sights in one-day cricket to have a hard chase highlighted by two flat throws at 150 kilometres per hour as the batsmen scramble to get home.

This tactic, which has been used in baseball for many years, is now an everyday part of the one-day game. Once batsmen started to run on balls being thrown in from the boundary because they knew they had the two or three seconds needed to get home safely, fielding teams had to come up with countermeasures. If a batsman plays a straight drive to the long boundary at the Adelaide Oval, for example, or the far-flung square boundaries at the MCG or the WACA, they know they have plenty of time to make their ground even if the fieldsman has the ball in his hand as they turn for the run.

The relay has proved to be the most effective way to counter this. In smart teams, a fieldsman will position himself between the stumps and the player chasing the ball as soon as a stroke is played towards a long boundary. It is exactly the same thing you see in baseball where hits of 100 metres or more are not uncommon. In baseball, as in cricket, it is rare that a player can throw 80 to 90 metres.

Tom Moody who, not surprisingly given his Scottish heritage and long frame, holds the world haggis-hurling record has one of the best arms in the game. He can routinely throw hard and fast from a 90-metre boundary – only one of a handful of players with the strength and skill to do that. Other players might throw the ball 70 metres, but if it has run out of steam by the time it arrives, or it hits the ground and dribbles towards the stumps over the last 20 metres, the batsmen are safe and can make their ground comfortably.

This is where the relay throw becomes so valuable. The fieldsman chasing the ball can throw faster because he does not need to wind up so much to carry the extra 30 or 40 metres. The second throw, if it comes in hard and flat, maintains the pressure on the batsmen.

Who should move into position to take the first throw? Obviously, a player with a strong arm should be the relay thrower. But the ever-changing nature of an innings means this task can never be delegated to just the one specific player. There are too many variables. The fielding team cannot guarantee the ball will go to the off-side rather than the leg-side, or straighter rather than squarer, so there is no point having one or two players with the specific task of becoming the relay thrower.

Like all facets of one-day cricket, every player on the field should be alert and ready to respond to every ball. Commonsense, though, will tell you that some boundaries are long enough to accommodate two throws, while others will be easily carried by one. The players with strong arms are likely to be fielding at cover and midwicket, so they are ideally positioned to make ground to a position between the chaser and the stumps. Practise this skill at training.

The relay fieldsman will probably find this is the only time in a match when he is required to take the ball in a stationary, or nearly stationary position, with his back to the play. He needs to be able to swivel and get the ball in quickly – a skill that can only be perfected by constant practice.

The relay also comes in useful when players with a weaker throwing arm are involved. Many players are superb fieldsman – David Gower springs to mind immediately – whose throwing ability was hampered by injury. Gower, the elegant England batsman, was like a cat in the infield who could get to the ball quicker than most players of his day. He could prevent it going through the infield or, if it did, was fleet-footed enough to stop it going to the boundary. Later in his career, though, he lost his once-powerful throwing arm and could not get the ball back quickly. England compensated for this by having a second fieldsman shadow Gower and get into position to take a short throw from him, then relay it directly to the keeper's or bowler's end.

Michael Bevan is another player who fits that category. Bevo is a superb fieldsman – he probably had no equal when he first arrived on the international scene – but while he retains the pace and balance that made him so formidable, injury has cost him some of the power in his throwing arm. Not having a bullet-like throw means Bevan will not always field in the ring where the fieldsman are constantly required to throw down the stumps with powerful returns to beat a batsman moving at full pace. Now, he often fields as a boundary rider because his pace enables him to cut off balls that other players would not be able to get to. But he can't get the ball back quickly, so Australia often has a relay player present himself halfway to the stumps to take Bevan's throw and send it back to the keeper. This takes full advantage of Bevan's foot-speed and puts the batsmen in two minds. They might well run on Bevan's arm, but they are less likely to do so if a player with a strong arm has the ball in hand from 40 or so metres and they are still only halfway down the pitch.

It is a sensible tactic and one that can be practised regularly by having players drop into the space between the stumps and the chaser. Remember, it is vital to talk to the fieldsman chasing to let him know the whereabouts of the relay man and the state of play with the batsmen. This means he has a good idea where the relayer is by the time he gets to the ball and can instantly whip it back to that fieldsman.

# Bounce Throw

The bounce throw is another tactic often used by the boundary riders to save time in getting the ball back to the stumps. A flat throw will often take less time to arrive than a loopy one, even if it bounces once or twice before getting in. The ball can also be easier to take if it bounces far enough in front of the waiting player.

Unfortunately, a ball that bounces only a metre or so in front of the receiver is the most difficult of all to take, especially on rough turf – the area around the stumps can often become rough later in an innings – so there is very little margin for error.

Bounce throws are also very useful late in the day when the sun is low in the sky. Plenty of fieldsmen will recall seeing the poor old keeper or bowler squinting into the sun as the ball comes in, wondering if it is coming at head height or at their ankles. If the throw lands ten metres short of the stumps and comes in low and hard, it makes the receiving job that much easier.

And if the ball is thrown into the sun, the offending fieldsman will soon get the message that he is putting his teammate's teeth and shins at risk. Better to throw low and not cop a spray.

# Slide

The slide is another technique that developed from one-day cricket and has entered all forms of the game. There is only one reason for this – it is effective and the test

169

of time has given it the thumbs up. No longer is sliding into position a lairy thing to do – people now realise it gives the fieldsman an invaluable advantage and saves those crucial hundredths and thousandths of a second that could be the difference between a run-out and a batsman getting home safely.

The key to one-day fielding success is quick release of the ball and there is no better way to demonstrate that than by picking the ball up in the same action as you prepare to throw. The key to the slide is to keep your eye on the ball and time your approach correctly. Running in the same direction as the ball, the trick is to draw almost level with it, then to drop down onto the side of your thigh – left leg if you are a right-hander or right leg if you are a leftie – so that you skid past the ball and gather it in with your hand as you slow down. Then, push your feet into the ground and drive back upright at the same time as winding up and preparing to throw. If done properly, you will be side-on to the target and can release the ball the instant you are back on your feet.

This manoeuvre can usually save at least a second or two compared with the orthodox fielding technique of chasing, stopping, turning around and throwing. It is a technique best suited to good outfields because there is less chance of the ball bouncing away from your grasp.

Mind you, there is little that looks as comical on the cricket field as a fieldsman who misjudges his slide and finds the ball has gone past him. This is not as uncommon as fieldsman hope, particularly on grounds such as the WACA which has such a fast outfield.

It happened to England all-rounder Mark Alleyne in Brisbane in January 1999. He was chasing a ball towards the line when he dropped into the slide. Unfortunately, he had not taken into account the speed of the outfield which

GOOD BALANCE AND WATCHING THE BALL ARE THE KEYS TO MASTERING THE SLIDE.
IT IS A VALUABLE FIELDING TECHNIQUE THAT WILL SAVE MANY RUNS IN THE FIELD.
PRACTISE IT AT TRAINING UNTIL YOU ARE CONFIDENT OF USING IT IN A MATCH.

171

took the ball away from him as he was about to grab it. It happened again a few metres further on and then again as Alleyne flailed in its wake. By the time the ball had slowed enough for him to grab it, there wasn't a hole deep enough for Alleyne to bury himself. To his credit, though, Alleyne didn't drop his head but fought back manfully and later produced a superb piece of fielding that ran out Shane Warne and virtually assured England's victory.

The slide is equally suited to the occasion when a player makes a last-ditch effort to stop the ball running into a fence. It is difficult, and dangerous, to run at full-tilt right up to the fence, yet few committed fieldsman are prepared to give up the chase if they have a chance of stopping the boundary. The slide can be used by the fieldsman to get into position to flick the ball back and then to use the legs to absorb the impact as he cannons into the pickets.

If you do this, it is essential to bend your knees and to hit the fence with the soles of your feet so the shock of impact is naturally absorbed by your flexed knees. If you do it right, you will save a run or two and won't suffer any injury worse than a grass stain on your trousers. Remember that it is essential to practise this hard at training.

Work on dropping onto your thigh and letting your momentum take you past the ball. It's not that smart to try to be a hero by sliding into a solid boundary to save four runs if you have never attempted the technique before.

A spontaneous slide might work, but you also might be like Queensland's gentle giant Carl Rackemann at the MCG the first time he tried a slide to save a boundary. Instead of going in feet-first, big Carl adopted a bodysurfing pose better suited to Scarborough or Bondi and careered head-first into the fence. It was a tough lesson for him, but an effective one.

# Walking In

'Walk in with the bowler,' coaches and coaching manuals drill endlessly. They emphasise the need to have momentum as you prepare to field. It is far easier to change direction or break into top pace if you are already on the move. Being balanced and mobile is essential if you are going to field well.

But in which direction should a player walk as he approaches the stumps? Boundary riders should move directly towards the batsman. Being so far from the bat, they have extra time to assess where a shot has been played and can move towards the ball's destination. So, too, the straight fieldsmen – mid-on and mid-off – who have a clear view of the batsman and can anticipate from the stroke where the ball will go. The mid-on and mid-off should move directly towards the bat and then go sideways if the shot goes straighter or wider.

Players who field in the squarer positions – cover point and square leg or midwicket – may not necessarily walk towards the batsman as all fieldsmen were once told. The best fieldsmen always seem to be able to find the straightest and therefore shortest line to the ball. Perhaps they see the ball before other players but it always seems that the players who have the greatest time to play the ball when they are batting – players like Viv Richards, Mark Waugh and David Gower – demonstrate the same attributes in the field by making the difficult seem easy and the impossible achievable.

They may gain some of their advantage by walking towards the middle of pitch or even the other stumps to cut down the angles. There is a good reason for that, of course. If you walk straight at the batsman, you will also be square on to the ball. It is easier to field the ball by being that fraction more side-on because it takes less time to get into position to stop it and then throw it back.

173

Square fieldsmen don't have to stay in the middle of the zone they have been assigned to cover. Rather, they can play a little more to one side to counter a batsman's strength or compensate for their own less favoured side. Imagine, say, Ricky Ponting fielding at midwicket to a right-handed batsman who likes to drive straight. Ponting will walk towards the middle of the pitch to improve the angle for straighter shots onto his left side. He will get to balls on his weaker side quicker, therefore gaining a fraction of a second, while not losing much on his stronger side. Of course, he will have a greater area to cover on his right side but being a right-hander, and naturally able to get to the ball faster and get rid of it faster, he can make up for the bigger zone. It is only a matter of a few degrees — a metre or two perhaps — but again it can save that millisecond that could be so vital.

This is another example of the battle within the battle — the one between the batsman and fieldsman. By gaining a fraction of a metre and a fraction of a second, the fieldsman can put doubts into the mind of his opponent. It might stop the batsman taking a sharp single, which is a small victory for the fielding team, or it might be a bigger win by creating a run-out chance.

# Backing Up

There is no secret to effective backing up in the field — it is simply a matter of commonsense. All fieldsmen need to be alert for every ball, but just because the ball is hit onto the leg-side, say, there is no reason for the players on the off-side to relax. Instead, they should immediately sum up the situation and prepare to back up the stumps. As the ball starts to fly around the field, particularly in the hit-or-miss last few overs of the innings, the numbers of throws at the stumps

174

increases dramatically. Not all of them can be stopped by the keeper or the man at the bowler's end either, meaning the fieldsmen in the ring have an important task to do.

They need to get into position and cover the throw in case it comes through. That means taking up station about 20 to 30 metres from the stumps and in a continuation of the line extending from the stumps to the fieldsman with the ball.

The depth is important because it gives the backing-up fieldsman time to move sideways if the throw is wide or if it deflects off the stumps or the man standing over them. Players should get into position at both ends to prevent an overthrow and then a second line of defence should be created by the players on the boundary. When they see the ball being played onto the other side of the field, the boundary riders should move in to provide another line behind the ring fieldsmen. This will stop an overthrow going for four, almost a capital offence in one-day cricket where most of the zones on the field are covered by at least one fieldsman. It can also save a single.

How many times do you see a batsman travelling at top pace to make a single, unable to slow down until he is ten metres or more past the stumps? In the time it takes him to slow, stop, turn around and get back to the crease, the ball could have travelled 60 metres into the outfield. If it is fielded quickly, it can be back to the stumps before the batsman is ready to run again. This gives extra protection to the player who fields the ball originally and allows him to have a shot at the stumps to try to get a run-out.

Like all parts of one-day cricket, teamwork is important. The pressure certainly builds on the batsmen if the fieldsmen are alert and get into position to cater for the shies at the stumps.

Wicketkeepers are not exempt from backing up, either. Often the keeper will not have time to get up to the stumps but will be able to move into position to back up if the ball is run into the close field. The wicketkeeper will often be in the play later in the game, particularly if the fine leg is on the fence and two men in the ring are in front of square leg. That means there is a large area without a close fieldsman that the keeper has to cover. And being the driving force of the fielding team, the keeper should ensure he tells the deep fieldsmen to come up to provide the second line of defence. Sharp fieldsmen will realise this automatically and get into position, but it does not harm to have a voice reminding all players to make sure they do the right thing.

**5**

# Captaincy

Captaining a cricket team is the easiest thing in the world – if you are sitting on the other side of the fence. If Australia, or any country for that matter, could pick its best captain, it would have a choice of millions. And it would never lose a game; it would take a wicket with every bowling change, and every batsman would score a century, having been placed in their rightful spot in the order.

Mind you, it would need much bigger change-rooms because the team would consist of at least 25 players, with another dozen or so pressing for selection. Come to think of it, captaining is pretty easy during the game, too.

All the captain has to do is win the toss, get his batsmen to score runs quickly and in great volume, then throw the ball to the bowlers who will run through the opposition. Oh, and don't forget, he will have placed a catcher in position for every ball that goes into the air. No wonder wicketkeepers are rarely appointed captain – imagine having to do all that and take each delivery, too.

Seriously though, the role of the captain carries enormous weight. He has to lead by example; inspire his troops when things are not going so well; keep a lid on the team if they are getting carried away at quick successes; wear the complaints of players who think they are not getting a go; and convince others who are weary or despondent to bowl another good spell or see off a hostile attack.

He has to be firm yet fair, instinctive yet disciplined, attacking yet defensive and able to listen to advice, but capable of making his own decisions. It is a hard job, yet the influence of a good captain can almost be measured on the scoreboard.

As is characteristic of one-day cricket, captains need to be versatile and able to follow their natural instincts. Captaining is also one of the areas of the game in which a person can learn most from experience or by observing someone else in action. But for all the watching and learning, a good captain needs his own spark and the confidence to back his own judgment.

The best player in the team is often appointed captain, though this practice is not followed to the letter. India, for example, found in 1998 that Sachin Tendulkar's game suffered when he was appointed captain. The team was not performing as it should, either. He was replaced by his predecessor, Mohammad Azharuddin, a talented and experienced skipper in his own right. Tendulkar responded with the most implacable onslaught one-day cricket has ever seen — nine centuries and 1834 runs in the year. Now he is back as skipper, so it will be fascinating to see if the responsibility affects his batting. I hope it does when we play India!

Good captains, like good teams, tend to be aggressive. If the opposition shows a weakness, they are quick to bore in to take advantage. Shane Warne, for example, is an aggressive captain with the extraordinary record of ten wins from the 11 matches in which he has captained Australia. Like Sir Donald Bradman, whose captaincy was boosted by the sharpest blade the game has ever seen — himself — Warne has an advantage

178

in being able to call on himself to get a breakthrough or slow the run rate.

But good captains know they have to temper aggression with commonsense. There is little point in using only three fieldsmen on the boundary in the last few overs if two batsmen are set on a flat pitch and are hitting the ball all over the ground. It is all very well to try things with the batting line-up by employing a pinch-hitter, say, but more often than not, the best batsmen batting as high in the order as possible will score most of the runs. A good captain will learn all of this and more as he gains experience and gets a feel for the tempo of the game.

A good captain will learn when to attack and when to set defensive fields in a bid to choke the run rate and build pressure on the batsmen. He will learn when to hold his nerve if one bowler is getting hit, but looks like taking a wicket; or when to surprise the opposition by opening with a spinner. Most importantly, and good captains must learn this if they are to succeed in one-day cricket, he will read the game and get a feeling for what will happen – an over or two before it does. This sort of skill comes with practice and from being in tune with the game.

Some captains have definite traits and others are predictable only in that they are unpredictable. All of them depend on their team to perform.

I have played under a series of one-day captains – Steve Waugh, Shane Warne, Mark Taylor, Ian Healy, Tom Moody, Damien Martyn, Phil Emery and Mark Lavender – with each of them demonstrating different characteristics.

I have probably played most matches under Steve, for Australia, and Tom, for WA. They share a few traits. Both have enormous experience – they have each played hundreds of one-day matches – and can be relied on to stay calm, no matter what is happening on the field. That is

179

not to say they won't express themselves if a player is not pulling his weight. They are both players who tend to lead by example.

Steve and Tom are not afraid to ask for suggestions. This doesn't mean they are short of an idea or two themselves – they just appreciate another point of view. This can be just an informal 'What do you reckon?' as we pass each other at the end of an over. But sometimes they will ask how a certain bowler is going, or request information about the pitch, or how a batsman is playing. This is where the wicketkeeper plays an important role in assessing players and being able to report to the skipper to help him make objective decisions.

Interestingly, both Steve and Tom are good one-day bowlers who are sometimes reluctant to use themselves. It is not uncommon that if they ask for a suggestion, I will respond: 'I reckon you should give yourself a bowl.' Now, before you think I am just trying to stay in their good books, I can assure you that sometimes captains will look at every other bowling option before themselves, so often a word or two doesn't go astray.

It is important for a captain to able to read what a batsman is intending to do so he can take countermeasures. He may push a fieldsman or two back to the boundary to block the expected onslaught of shots. Or he may consider that an aggressive batsman who has struck a few over the infield is playing with fire and is likely to get out if he continues in that vein. In this situation, the captain might decide to leave the field in and rely on the bowler hitting the spot. He might think if he puts the fieldsmen back, the pressure has been relieved and the batsman might not take a risk now, he will simply push the ball along the ground. That is a matter of experience and of reading the play.

After 20 overs or so, the captain should have a good idea of how the pitch is playing, how well the batsmen are going, and what sort of job his bowlers are doing. At this stage, he should consider what sort of target the opposition are likely to get and decide how he is going to play it. He might think that a wicket or two is needed because the batsmen are getting away. Or he might be happy with the way things are going and concentrate on keeping the runs to a manageable level. Balance and timing are the keys.

There are many variables. Working out where each fits into the overall scheme will only come with practice and observation. Taking wickets will slow the run rate, but having aggressive bowlers in action with attacking fields will allow runs to be scored. On the other hand, being too defensive could allow the batsmen to take four or five singles an over and build their momentum that way. It is important that the captain and his bowlers, fieldsmen and batsmen work as a team and that each player is aware of the task required of him.

The vice-captain also has a role to play, particularly when the team is fielding. In this case, it is important that the deputy keeps track of the overs bowled by each player so that planning in the last few overs, when things are usually at their most frantic, can be maintained with as few dramas as possible. Tom Moody will sometimes say at the 40-over mark, when the shape of the innings has become apparent, that he is thinking of using certain bowlers at the end. He might then say: 'I am thinking of BJ and Jo Angel for the last five overs. How am I going with them?'

This means he needs to know the earliest point at which they can come back, or whether there needs to be any shuffling of bowlers to achieve that plan. If he is concentrating on setting fields, which can take up most, if not all, of his attention during the last few overs, it becomes important for his deputy to add up the sums and keep him up to date. It is a small thing, but it could be vital.

# Field Positions

Placing the field is one of the most basic tasks in cricket. It is the first thing, apart from choosing which bowlers to use, a captain has to consider when he walks onto the field for the start of an innings. It can have a huge impact on the game. Watch any good one-day captain in the field and you will see him spending considerable time making sure the fieldsmen are set in the right position. Is the deep player on the cover boundary too square, or should he be set straighter? Does the midwicket need to come in a few metres to reduce the chance of a quick single? Do we need a slip and a gully or would a second slip and a short cover be a better option?

A good captain or bowler will have a picture in his mind of the fields he wants to set at various times of the innings. He will tend to be more attacking at the start and concentrate more on defence at the end. But one-day cricket is a game of flexibility, so the fields will change often. Sometimes, they will change at every ball, particularly in a tense run chase when two different types of batsmen are at the crease – adjustments have to be made after every change of strike.

If a left-handed batsman such as Michael Bevan, who will mainly look to work the ball around by piercing the field for ones and twos, is batting with right-handed Brendon Julian, a strong hitter who will look for boundaries rather than quick singles, the captain will be constantly changing players in a bid to frustrate the batsmen and restrict their scoring options. Fieldsmen need to be alert in this situation, knowing that they can be called on to move every minute or so. They will do the team a favour by being ready to go, then quickly getting into position. It is frustrating for the fielding team, and can be inspiring to the batsmen, to have fieldsmen moving slowly and dragging their feet. It is much better to be alert, quick and vigorous so that the batsmen have little time to relax.

As discussed in the chapter on fielding, it is important to have the right players in the positions that best suit their abilities. The best fieldsman will invariably field at point. It is the place that Jonty Rhodes has made his own. Ricky Ponting fields there, too. It is no coincidence. The attributes needed at point are speed, sharp reflexes and a great arm. It is a versatile position where the fieldsman has to stop full-blooded shots one ball, then dash in at full pace the next when the batsmen has dropped the ball at his feet and set off for a quick single. Catches will also come there, sometimes a savage square cut travelling above head height or towards the feet, or a lob off the leading edge that hovers in the air and forces the player to stretch at top pace. Speed is crucial, as is throwing strength and accuracy.

In virtually every game, the man at point will have the chance to throw down the stumps. My very first match as an opener for Australia showed me how critical a good point fieldsman can be, and how he can build the pressure that leads to a wicket.

The best catchers will go to slip or the close-in positions. Usually on Australia's bouncier wickets, the catchers will be at slip. But this is not always the case. Sometimes a captain might want to use a short cover or short midwicket as a catcher and as a player who doubles up to stop short singles.

Mark Taylor, one of the best slips fieldsmen of all time, regularly snapped up great catches at midwicket. And Mark Waugh, who seems to have glue on his hands when he is standing at second slip or silly point in Test matches, is the same in the close positions in front of the wicket.

You knew as a batsman not to hit the ball in the air anywhere near that pair or you wouldn't be long at the crease. The catching restriction, which means two fieldsmen must be within 15 yards of the bat for the first

15 overs, has also led to the development of innovative tactics. For example, it is rare in the subcontinent that two slips will stay in after five overs. The pitches keep much lower and are less likely to allow the bowler to catch the edges. Short cover and short midwicket will often come into play almost from the start.

In India and Pakistan, another tactic is to take out the fine leg and bring him up to a catching position at leg slip. He is not just there for the edge, but to exploit the rules and enable an extra run saver in the ring. You know that if the bowler sticks to the right line (i.e. outside off-stump), the leg slip will hardly come into the game. In this case, the captain prefers to have an extra fieldsman in the ring, say at cover, but is still able to abide by the rules.

However, there is one situation that allows the catchers to go deeper than 15 yards from the bat when they are at a legitimate slip position. There was an innovation in Australia last season that recognised the slips will sometimes field deeper than 15 yards, but will still be in a legitimate catching position. If, for example, Glenn McGrath or Allan Donald is bowling, it would be suicide for a slip to be too close. I often stand back 20 metres or more to the quicks and the slips are even deeper. The same applies to leg slip. The cricket authorities have recognised this by having dots on the field to mark 15 yards from the bat – so that the players in front or square of the wicket don't go too deep.

It is also important that the captain stays in the ring. If he goes outside, it is harder to see what is happening and almost impossible to consult with the bowler and keeper. Allan Border, for example, made midwicket his position and Steve Waugh often fields at square leg or mid-on. Players such as Courtney Walsh and Arjuna Ranatunga, who aren't particularly mobile, will field in the ring. They might miss a run or two because they are not as nimble as some other players, but they compensate enough by being close to the action.

# Field Restrictions

Field restrictions order two catching fieldsmen to be in position for the first 15 overs while only two players are allowed outside the 30-yard circle during that time. After 15 overs, only five are allowed outside the circle.

These restrictions have been a great innovation, preventing fielding teams from being ultra-defensive and encouraging the spectacle of big hitting. In 1998/99, the domestic one-day competition took that restriction a step further by only allowing one extra fieldsman outside the circle between overs 16 and 30. This may also prove to be a success, but it probably won't have the same impact as the introduction of the 30-yard zone.

The restrictions mean captains have to give special thought to how they attack in the opening overs. When I walk out to bat, unorthodox fields are often set for me as fielding captains try to combat what they see as my strengths. In my case, the fine leg often comes inside the ring and a player goes back to the fence at deep backward square. This tactic acknowledges that I hit a lot of pull shots – it is better value to restrict that avenue of my batting than trying the conservative approach of having a traditional fine leg.

# The First 15 Overs

An orthodox start for the fast bowler is to have two slips and one gully, point, mid-off, mid-on, square leg, fine leg and third man.

The third man is vital in one-day games and will be in the game from the start – as a definite run saver and sometimes as a catcher. The batsmen go harder at the

# FAST BOWLER: OVERS 1–15

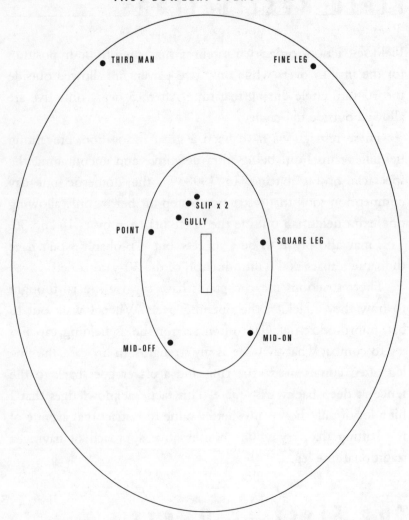

ball early on, so they have more chance of getting edges and going over or wide of the slips. As there are less slips than in a four-day match, there is less chance of stopping the ball anyway.

Batsmen will also often glide the ball to third man. All good one-day players have that shot as part of their game. It has a low element of risk due to the lack of slips, and it is essential in turning over the strike and keeping the score going. In fact, you could describe it as the classic one-day shot. Where bowlers have a stock ball, the batsman has that as a stock shot. He can play it to a ball of any length and though he is not looking for a boundary, he knows he has an easy single there.

So, third man is a key position because it is in the play so often. The third man fieldsman needs to have a good throwing arm, as does everyone who regularly fields on the boundary, and he has to be quick to the ball because he is covering such a huge area. He also needs good catching hands, because on some grounds – such as the WACA or Brisbane with their bouncy pitches – the ball will often fly from cuts or top edges and carry to the fence.

The effectiveness of third man as a catching position was never more evident than at the 1996 World Cup semi-final between India and Sri Lanka in Calcutta. Sri Lanka were batting and, as usual, openers Romesh Kaluwitharana and Sanath Jayasuriya planned to blaze away at anything short and take the risk of hitting in the air. But both players were out in the first over of the day when they slashed short balls from Javagal Srinath straight down the throat of the third man.

I suffered a similar fate in the World Cup semi-final at Edgbaston, and also in the West Indies in April 1999. In the match at Barbados, I slashed the second ball I received, a short delivery from Merv Dillon over backward point for six. 'You beauty,' I thought. 'Today's the day for a big score.'

These thoughts grew stronger when I saw the same delivery come my way two balls later. How wrong I was! I played the same shot, but the ball bounced a little more than the previous ball. Instead of coming out of the meat of the bat, it took the top edge and flew straight into the waiting hands of Curtly Ambrose, who did not have to take a step down at deep third man. Out for 6 in four balls. It was a pretty good strike rate but it wasn't really the start the team was after . . .

It's important to remember not to play right on the boundary but to be prepared to come in ten metres or more. The old rule that you have to start on the fence plays little part in one-day cricket. Batsmen are so good at running between wickets and taking the pace off the ball that they will often get two rather than one for a shot that goes to the boundary fieldsman.

The deep fieldsman must be able to get in quickly to cut off the second run. That would be almost impossible if the fieldsman was on the fence at a big ground such as the WACA or the MCG. But don't get too close in or the most important role of the position – to stop boundaries – is restricted. The same applies at long-on or long-off where you need to play in from the boundary a bit to stop the batsmen taking two.

With the close-in field at the start of the innings, the point fieldsman is probably the only one to start outside the circle. Mid-off and mid-on need to be in to stop the single, while the fieldsmen in the squarer positions stand further towards the circle, but are still ready to come in to prevent ones. Towards the end of the innings, fieldsmen will start from further back to have a greater chance of stopping boundaries rather than ones. They will start walking from outside the circle so that they are just inside when the bowler delivers. This is only for late in the day when they are trying to stop boundaries and twos or threes.

The best catchers go to slips, while fieldsmen with the least powerful arm will mostly stay in the ring. As in all forms of cricket, fine leg can be used for the most lumbering fieldsman, such as ungainly quick bowlers who are not too quick across the turf.

Selecting the right player to field at cover or midwicket is very important. In fact, depending on the batsman, it could be vital. Some players will loft the ball through midwicket, so it is important to have a good catcher there. Allan Border used to field there and took many great catches.

Mark Taylor, too, has taken a few rippers at short midwicket. The key is to have safe hands and to be agile. The man at short midwicket does not have to be as quick as the man at point – they tend to be closer to the bat, and the batsmen are less likely to hit to them and run.

Ricky Ponting doesn't always field at point for every ball during a match. On occasions, he moves to midwicket as part of a specific tactical ploy designed to use his athleticism and deadly throwing arm to Australia's advantage. This ploy takes place when Shane Warne is bowling and Ponting becomes the only fieldsman inside the ring on the leg-side.

'Shane likes me on the leg-side where there are no other fieldsmen,' Ponting explained after his tremendous match against Sri Lanka in Perth in January 1999, when he took a wicket, two sharp catches, threw down the stumps and stopped everything that came near him.

The tactical thinking is simple. Ponting is fast so he is capable of covering a wide space and stopping plenty of balls that are pushed into the leg-side. And his uncanny ability to get run-outs with direct hits and returns directly beside the stumps makes batsmen wary of running when the ball is in his vicinity. It is almost like having an extra fieldsman in the ring. This means Warne can be more attacking by bowling at the stumps, rather than just on or outside off-stump. He knows he will not be picked off for a single through the leg-side. It is a superb example of a partnership between a bowler and fieldsman and the subtle influence their relationship can have on the game.

# 16 to 50 overs

Fifteen overs have been completed. The deep square leg goes out and one probably goes back to the straight boundary. It becomes a pretty standard field and won't change much from overs 16 to 50, except that one or two might drop back to boundary. Often, teams will play out the last few overs with the fine leg up and five fieldsmen in the deep for the big hit. Of course, it is crucial that the bowler bowls the right line.

There is probably nothing more frustrating in the game than to have a batsman glance a ball from just outside leg-stump when the fine leg has just come up. The ball goes to the boundary and the captain pulls his hair out. And if it is annoying when the batsman French-cuts it, imagine what it feels like if it is the result of a loose ball down the leg-side.

It makes batting tactics interesting, though. Take, for example, New Zealander Dion Nash in Australia in 1997/98. He started to play shots from outside-off to go to fine leg. He didn't hit across the line – he put the bat on an angle and virtually scooped the ball from outside-off to the leg-side. The shot brought him plenty of runs and nearly won a game against South Africa in Brisbane in January 1998. The Kiwis needed 25 runs off the last two overs to overhaul South Africa's massive total of 300 before Nash and Daniel Vettori got it down to seven off two balls. Nash played a superb shot from the second-last ball – paddling the Shaun Pollock delivery from the stumps and high over fine leg.

New Zealand thought it was home because the ball hit the deeper of two boundary ropes which had been separated during the night and were sitting 30 centimetres apart. But the umpires thwarted their hopes, deeming it only to be a four. Nash was caught on the boundary from the next ball to give South Africa victory by two runs and set an Australian record for the combined total of 598 runs.

It was an audacious stroke by Nash and one that effectively circumvented the captain's fielding plan. But it was a rare victory, too, and a risk the fielding captain will usually take because he knows that if the bowlers put the ball on the right spot, the batsman will more than likely play in front or square of the wicket where the field is set.

Sweepers on the boundary line are now standard and depending on the situation, the men in the ring might field right on the 30-yard line to stop twos, or they might come in to prevent ones. Say a good hitter is on strike. You might prefer to allow him to take one so you can pressure the non-striker who might be a lesser batsman or new to the crease. The players on the fence have to be alert, though, especially in the last few overs, because the batsmen will be looking for two even if it goes straight to them. It is the batsmen's way of putting pressure on the field and trying to force a misfield. The fieldsman can do the same to the batsmen by getting the ball quickly and returning it swiftly.

After 15 overs, it is rare that three or even four fieldsmen won't be in the deep. The batting team would have to be 5–30 or in similar trouble to change that tactic. However, just because the 15 is up, a captain might not necessarily put the men out immediately. The game is flexible and a good captain stays in tune with it. He assesses it as he goes along and if he feels he can attack a new batsman or put pressure on one who has been batting for a while, he will do so.

In the subcontinent, batsmen invariably score quickest in the first 15 overs when the ball is hard and the field is in. Things are slightly different in Australia because the grassy outfields and less abrasive pitches allow the ball to retain its hardness longer. The principle of batsmen attacking early is still in place, though, so a fielding team will often approach a match with the intention of putting as much defensive pressure on early, because they know the batsmen will play big shots right from the start.

The Sri Lankans are like that. They try to get off to a blazing start then consolidate in the second half of the innings, knowing that with the field out and plenty of gaps in the infield, they will be able to score at four an over without too many risks. They have used that game plan for three or four years. It doesn't work all the time, but it does pay off often enough for them to stick with it.

So, defensive countermeasures are required early in the innings to stop the onslaught. Players in the ring will field right on the line, the two deep men will be employed squarer to cover more space and perhaps the two catchers will be placed in 'dummy' positions where they can double up as run savers. That is why you will sometimes see a leg slip in place and no fine leg – the captain is meeting the requirement of the fielding restrictions by having the leg slip as a catcher simply to allow another fieldsman to be positioned in the ring to stop one. Of course, with the fine leg moved to deep square leg, say, there is no room for the bowler to stray down the leg-side.

It's fine to bowl a spinner early, too. Shane Warne often bowls early. Mark Taylor used to do it a lot, and Steve Waugh also will bring on Warne early, especially if the batsmen have got off to a flying start. They turn to Warne because of his wicket-taking ability. It may be a big risk with the spin bowler not having a lot of protection, but the best way to slow the run rate is to get a wicket. Warne is a special case because he is so accurate and can be relied on to bowl on one side of the wicket. But the principle remains the same: a spinner brought on early can do a lot of good.

Look at Dipak Patel in the World Cup in 1992 or Pat Symcox in Australia in 1998. In many teams, it is quite feasible that the best bowler will be a spinner and it makes sense to get them on early so that they can have the other team on the back-foot. It makes less sense for the best bowler to come on when the opposition is 1–120 after 25 overs and building a big total.

# LEG-SPINNER: OVERS 1–15

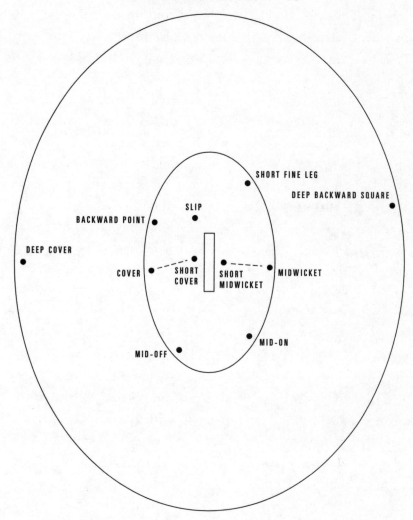

If the ball is not turning a lot, the deep cover might come in and the mid-on can be pushed back to long-on. The leggie will have to bowl at off-stump and try to get the batsman to play straight. If he needs protection because the batsman is punishing him through the off-side, the short cover can be pushed out to the ring – which means

193

CAPTAINCY

## LEG-SPINNER: OVERS 16-50

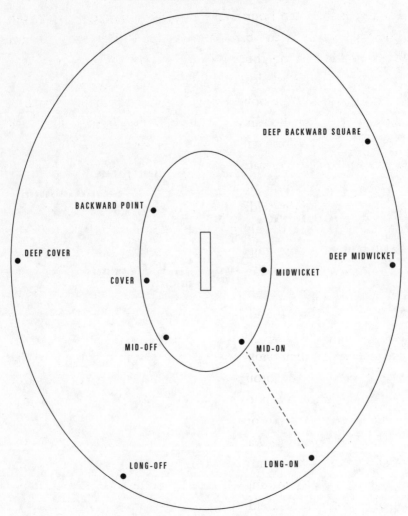

another catcher has to come in. The backward square could come up to leg slip. He might not be in the play much, particularly if the bowler is bowling to a good off-stump attack, but it means the 15-over restrictions are met. It's a fairly orthodox field with a standard ring in the circle and a deep cover outside.

As the innings progresses, the leg-spinner will push fieldsmen back to protect the boundaries. Five men may stay on the off-side, particularly if the ball is turning. It is likely he will have three in the ring on the off-side with just the one position – midwicket – covered close on the leg-side. The captain needs to be flexible, but if the bowler can maintain his line of just on or outside off-stump, he can get away with just the two on the off-side boundary. This will allow three men on the leg-side boundary to cover, or catch, the big shot played to leg.

Batsmen will often play unorthodox shots to this sort of field to counter the tight fielding positions. Reverse sweeps are likely, especially if there is only the one fieldsman behind square on the off-side. Or they might sweep against the spin from outside off-stump, as Nasser Hussain and Graeme Hick did during the one-day series in Australia in 1999. The pair became tied down by Warne's accuracy and tried to combat it by sweeping from outside-off. They hit the ball in the air often, but they predetermined their shots knowing there was no catcher on the ring. If a player was brought up from the boundary, or one on the off-side was taken over to a short backward square, they would play in a more orthodox manner while having another gap to pick. Even so, Warne was not too concerned about the shot because it rarely brought a boundary and put the batsman at risk of getting a leading edge and popping a catch back to the bowler or into the infield.

It is not unusual for the off-spinner to come on in the first 15, or even open the bowling. It is a good tactic when the opposition batsmen have a history of launching an immediate assault on the fast bowlers and trying to hit over the top. There are many opening batsmen who are more comfortable with the ball coming through quickly than they are with a slower ball that forces them to wait and adjust their shot. Most famously, as discussed on page 92 of the

# OFF-SPINNER: OVERS 1–15

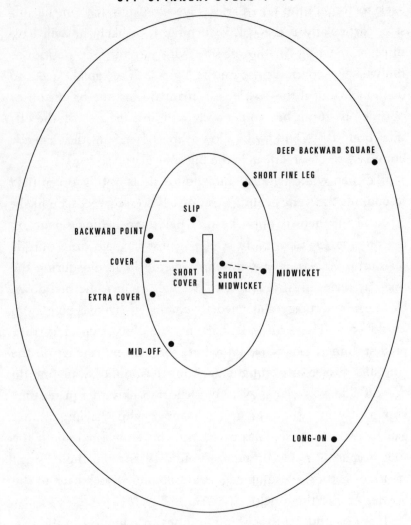

Bowling chapter, Dipak Patel opened in the 1992 World Cup for New Zealand when Kiwi skipper Martin Crowe came up with some innovative and daring strategies. Crowe thought that if the batting team was going to attack from the start, why not use a traditional defensive weapon at the beginning as well.

The off-spinner is not wholly defensive, of course, because a fresh wicket with a bit of life will give the spinner bounce and turn that might be gone after an hour or two. The off-side field will be a traditional ring, so it is important that it is staggered. That means one or two of the fieldsmen will be in to stop the one while the others will go back to the 30-yard line to stop harder shots.

The backward point will come in, likewise the cover, while the point will be right on line. Mid-off will start deep because he is covering a big area. He will also come into the game if the batsman tries to hit in the air down the ground and mistimes it or even hits it well, but low and in the air. The cover will be straighter rather than squarer, because there is already protection square of the wicket. And again, he will be walking towards the middle of the pitch, knowing that if the bowler hits the right line and length, the ball is more likely to be hit straight. That means he will be running in to cut it off at an angle and will be ready to throw at either wicket.

This tactic can put doubt into the batsman's mind if he has played an off-drive that could normally bring him a single with the mid-off set back on the line. This time, though, the batsman has to wait for the ball to pass the cover fieldsman before he can set off for a single.

It is vital that the fieldsmen are positioned correctly so that they can cross the path of the ball and keep the batsman wondering. The short cover might even come into a catching position, depending on conditions and the way the batsman is playing, pushing the short midwicket back into the ring. This is probably the only major change to the field, apart from the normal adjustments that will take place to make sure the fieldsmen are in the right places and that they aren't in line. Like all one-day fields, the deep men provide cover for the shorter ones – the theory is that if it gets past

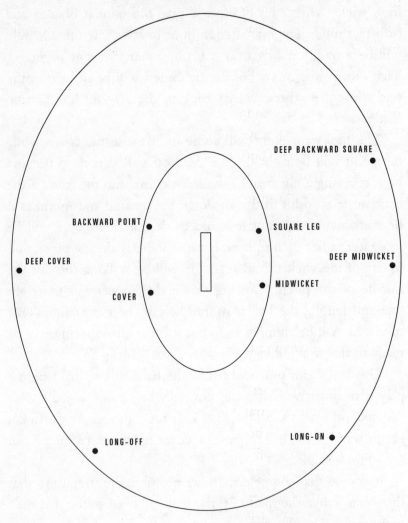

the closer man, the deeper one will be in a position to race around and stop the boundary. That, of course, doesn't always happen, but the percentages will pay off if the theory is applied correctly.

The bowler will be concentrating on an off-stump line knowing that there is plenty of room on the leg-side for the batsman to take a single or two if he strays and bowls on the middle or leg-stumps. He will bowl full and straight, but vary his pace just as he would during any other time during the innings.

It is imperative the off-spinner bowls straight. He will have five fieldsmen out, with the deep men virtually forming a defence zone in the middle of the batsman's likely hitting area. The use of only five players outside the circle means that not all areas can be covered, but again, if the percentages are right, the fieldsmen will be where the ball goes more often than not.

The orthodox position is one in, one out, right around the oval. The only boundary areas not covered are from behind the keeper through to deep cover, but that should not come into play if the bowler sticks to his full length and brings his line over more towards middle- and leg-stumps during the later overs of his spell. He will also bowl flatter and take less risks. That forces the batsman to take risks to hit through the off-side and allows the three men deep on the leg-side to stop the big hits.

Of course, this sort of field, again, makes shots like the reverse sweep more attractive – if the batsman can play it well, there is no one on the boundary to stop the four.

Mid-on and mid-off can be set wider than normal, with the deep men being placed straighter so they are between the infielders and the bowler. The bowler has plenty of work to do getting across to stop drives, or at least put enough doubt in the batsman's mind to slow him down enough for the deep men to come in and prevent two. That is just one of the many tiny pieces of teamwork that can have an influence on the way the game is played.

It might only influence the game by 1 per cent, but if enough of those 1 percenters are achieved, they can add up to a significant piece of play that could cause a

# FAST BOWLER: OVERS 16-50

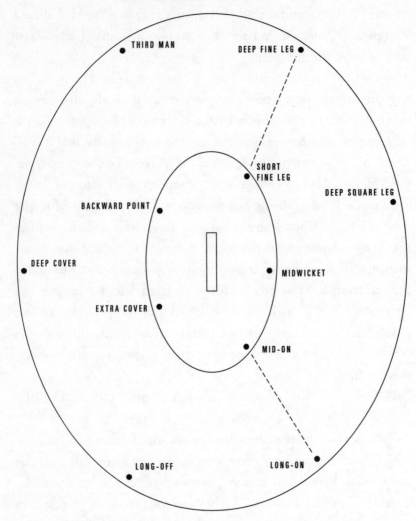

run-out or prevent the extra run that might be the difference between winning and losing. There is no catcher and the men in the ring will tend to play deeper later in the innings and closer earlier on when they are trying to stop singles.

Captains are born – and made. They need to have good leadership skills, a strong personality and be ready to lead by example. They also need to be able to learn. A captain who is inflexible and set in his ways will not get the best out of his team. On the other hand, a captain who looks and listens, who examines the many different circumstances thrown up during a one-day match and works at analysing the best means of handling those situations must be capable of striking hard when the game calls for it, and knowing when to throttle back a bit and stay calm in the face of adversity.

Captains get plenty of bouquets when things are going well but they also cop a few brickbats. As mentioned throughout this book, one of Steve Waugh's favourite pieces of advice is to back yourself and follow your instincts. I think that is pretty good advice for players and there is no reason it should not also apply to captains.

# Adam Gilchrist - Statistics

## Matches

| No. | Opponent | Location | Date | Score | c/st |
|-----|----------|----------|------|-------|------|
| 1 | South Africa | Faridabad | 25/10/96 | 18 | 2/- |
| 2 | South Africa | Gauteng | 1/11/96 | 0 | - |
| 3 | South Africa | East London | 29/3/97 | 1 | 1/1 |
| 4 | South Africa | Pt Elizabeth | 31/3/97 | dnb | - |
| 5 | South Africa | Durban | 5/4/97 | 77 | - |
| 6 | South Africa | Jo'burg | 8/4/97 | 26 | - |
| 7 | South Africa | Pretoria | 10/4/97 | 20* | - |
| 8 | South Africa | Bl'fontein | 13/4/97 | 3 | 1/- |
| 9 | England | The Oval | 24/5/97 | 53 | - |
| 10 | England | Lord's | 25/5/97 | 33 | - |
| 11 | South Africa | Sydney | 4/12/97 | 4 | 1/- |
| 12 | New Zealand | Adelaide | 7/12/97 | 29 | 1/- |
| 13 | South Africa | Melbourne | 9/12/97 | 29* | 1/1 |
| 14 | New Zealand | Melbourne | 17/12/97 | 11* | 3/- |
| 15 | South Africa | Brisbane | 11/1/98 | 21 | - |
| 16 | New Zealand | Sydney | 14/1/98 | 28 | 1/- |
| 17 | South Africa | Perth | 18/1/98 | 6 | - |
| 18 | New Zealand | Melbourne | 21/1/98 | dnb | 1/- |
| 19 | South Africa | Melbourne | 23/1/98 | 20 | 2/2 |
| 20 | South Africa | Sydney | 26/1/98 | 100 | 1/- |
| 21 | South Africa | Sydney | 27/1/98 | 6 | 1/2 |
| 22 | New Zealand | C'church | 8/2/98 | 118 | - |
| 23 | New Zealand | Wellington | 10/2/98 | 0 | 1/1 |
| 24 | New Zealand | Napier | 12/2/98 | 40 | 1/- |
| 25 | New Zealand | Auckland | 14/2/98 | 42 | 1/- |
| 26 | India | Cochin | 1/4/98 | 61 | 1/- |

# Matches – *continued*

| No. | Opponent | Location | Date | Score | c/st |
|-----|----------|----------|------|-------|------|
| 27 | Zimbabwe | Motera | 3/4/98 | 12 | 2/– |
| 28 | India | Kanpur | 7/4/98 | 11 | 1/– |
| 29 | Zimbabwe | Delhi | 11/4/98 | 1 | – |
| 30 | India | Delhi | 14/4/98 | 1 | 2/– |
| 31 | New Zealand | Sharjah | 18/4/98 | 57 | 1/– |
| 32 | India | Sharjah | 19/4/98 | 25 | 2/1 |
| 33 | New Zealand | Sharjah | 21/4/98 | 11* | 1 |
| 34 | India | Sharjah | 22/4/98 | 11 | 2/– |
| 35 | India | Sharjah | 24/4/98 | 45 | 2/– |
| 36 | India | Dhaka | 28/10/98 | 25 | 2/– |
| 37 | Pakistan | Karachi | 6/11/98 | 45 | 1/– |
| 38 | Pakistan | Peshawar | 8/11/98 | 42 | – |
| 39 | Pakistan | Lahore | 10/11/98 | 103 | 1/– |
| 40 | England | Brisbane | 10/1/99 | 13 | 3/– |
| 41 | Sri Lanka | Sydney | 13/1/99 | 131 | 3/– |
| 42 | England | Melbourne | 15/1/99 | 21 | 3/– |
| 43 | England | Sydney | 17/1/99 | 6 | 2/– |
| 44 | Sri Lanka | Hobart | 21/1/99 | 12 | – |
| 45 | Sri Lanka | Adelaide | 24/1/99 | 41 | 2/– |
| 46 | Sri Lanka | England | 26/1/99 | 0 | 1/– |
| 47 | Sri Lanka | Perth | 31/1/99 | 47 | 1/– |
| 48 | England | Sydney | 5/2/99 | 19 | 3/– |
| 49 | Sri Lanka | Melbourne | 7/2/99 | 154 | 2/– |
| 50 | England | Sydney | 10/2/99 | 29 | 2/1 |
| 51 | England | Melbourne | 13/2/99 | 52 | 4/– |
| 52 | West Indies | Arnos Vale | 11/4/99 | 2 | –/1 |
| 53 | West Indies | St George's | 14/4/99 | 17 | – |
| 54 | West Indies | Port–Spain | 17/4/99 | 43 | – |
| 55 | West Indies | Port–Spain | 18/4/99 | 25 | 1/– |

## Matches *– continued*

| No. | Opponent | Location | Date | Score | c/st |
|-----|----------|----------|------|-------|------|
| 56 | West Indies | Georgetown | 21/4/99 | 44 | –/1 |
| 57 | West Indies | Bridgetown | 25/4/99 | 64 | 2/1 |
| 58 | West Indies | Bridgetown | 26/4/99 | 6 | 2/– |
| 59 | Scotland | Worcester | 16/5/99 | 6 | 2/1 |
| 60 | New Zealand | Cardiff | 20/5/99 | 14 | 1/– |
| 61 | Pakistan | Leeds | 23/5/99 | 0 | 2/– |
| 62 | Bangladesh | Ch-Le-Str* | 27/5/99 | 63 | – |
| 63 | West Indies | Manchester | 30/5/99 | 21 | – |
| 64 | India | The Oval | 4/6/99 | 31 | 4/– |
| 65 | Zimbabwe | Lord's | 9/6/99 | 10 | 1/1 |
| 66 | South Africa | Leeds | 13/6/99 | 5 | – |
| 67 | South Africa | Birm'ham | 17/6/99 | 20 | – |
| 68 | Pakistan | Lord's | 20/6/99 | 54 | 2/– |
| 69 | Sri Lanka | Galle | 22/8/99 | 27 | 2/– |
| 70 | India | Galle | 23/8/99 | 68 | 1/– |
| 71 | Sri Lanka | Colombo | 26/8/99 | 38 | 1/2 |
| 72 | India | Colombo | 28/8/99 | 77 | 3/– |
| 73 | Sri Lanka | Colombo | 31/8/99 | 21 | 1/– |

\* *Chester Le Street*

## Opponents

| | m | i | no | r | hs | ave | 100 | 50 | 0 | c/st |
|---|---|---|----|----|----|-----|-----|----|----|------|
| South Africa | 17 | 16 | 2 | 356 | 100 | 25.42 | 1 | 1 | 1 | 10/6 |
| New Zealand | 11 | 10 | 2 | 350 | 118 | 43.75 | 1 | 1 | 1 | 11/2 |
| India | 10 | 10 | – | 355 | 77 | 35.50 | – | 3 | – | 20/2 |
| England | 9 | 9 | – | 226 | 53 | 25.11 | – | 2 | 1 | 18/1 |
| West Indies | 8 | 8 | – | 222 | 64 | 27.75 | – | 1 | – | 5/3 |
| Sri Lanka | 7 | 7 | – | 450 | 154 | 64.29 | 2 | – | – | 12/2 |
| Pakistan | 5 | 5 | – | 244 | 103 | 48.80 | 1 | 1 | 1 | 6/– |
| Zimbabwe | 3 | 3 | – | 23 | 12 | 7.66 | – | – | – | 3/1 |
| Scotland | 1 | 1 | – | 6 | 6 | 6.00 | – | – | – | 2/1 |
| Bangladesh | 1 | 1 | – | 66 | 66 | 66.00 | 1 | – | – | – |
| **TOTAL** | **73** | **71** | **4** | **2316** | **154** | **34.56** | **5** | **10** | **4** | **87/18** |

# In Australia

| | m | i | no | r | hs | ave | 100 | 50 | 0 | c/st |
|---|---|---|---|---|---|---|---|---|---|---|
| Sydney | 8 | 8 | – | 323 | 131 | 40.36 | 2 | – | – | 14/3 |
| Melbourne | 7 | 6 | 2 | 287 | 154 | 71.75 | 1 | 1 | – | 16/3 |
| Adelaide | 3 | 3 | – | 70 | 41 | 23.33 | – | – | 1 | 4/- |
| Brisbane | 2 | 2 | – | 34 | 21 | 17.00 | – | – | – | 3/- |
| Perth | 2 | 2 | – | 53 | 47 | 26.50 | – | – | – | 1/- |
| Hobart | 1 | 1 | – | 12 | 12 | 12.00 | – | – | – | – |
| **Sub-total** | **23** | **22** | **2** | **779** | **154** | **38.95** | **3** | **1** | **1** | **38/6** |

# Overseas

| | m | i | no | r | hs | ave | 100 | 50 | 0 | c/st |
|---|---|---|---|---|---|---|---|---|---|---|
| England | 12 | 12 | – | 310 | 54 | 25.83 | – | 2 | 1 | 12/2 |
| India | 7 | 7 | – | 104 | 61 | 14.85 | – | 1 | 1 | 8/- |
| West Indies | 7 | 7 | – | 201 | 64 | 28.71 | – | 1 | – | 5/3 |
| South Africa | 6 | 5 | 1 | 127 | 77 | 31.75 | – | 1 | – | 2/1 |
| Sri Lanka | 5 | 5 | – | 231 | 77 | 46.20 | – | 2 | – | 8/3 |
| Sharjah | 5 | 5 | 1 | 149 | 57 | 37.25 | – | 1 | – | 7/2 |
| New Zealand | 4 | 4 | – | 200 | 118 | 50.00 | 1 | – | 1 | 3/1 |
| Pakistan | 3 | 3 | – | 190 | 103 | 63.33 | 1 | – | – | 2/- |
| Bangladesh | 1 | 1 | – | 25 | 25 | 25.00 | – | – | – | 2/- |
| **Sub-total** | **50** | **49** | **2** | **1537** | **118** | **32.70** | **2** | **9** | **3** | **49/12** |
| **TOTAL** | **73** | **71** | **4** | **2316** | **154** | **34.56** | **5** | **10** | **4** | **87/12** |